EMANATIONS FROM THE PENUMBRA

poems

EMANATIONS

from the

PENUMBRA

poems

E.M. SCHORB

HILL HOUSE · NEW YORK

©2017, E.M. Schorb. All rights reserved.
Cover painting "O Carib Isle" by the Author

ISBN: 978-0-692-03402-6

Acknowledgements

Grateful acknowledgement is given the following publications in which some of these poems first appeared:

5 A.M., Agenda (UK), The American Scholar, Anthology of Magazine Verse & Yearbook of American Poetry, Antioch Review, The Arkansas Review, The Arts Journal, Atlanta Review, Bitterroot, Blood and Fire Review, Brink Literary Magazine, The Brownstone Review, The Cape Rock, The Carolina Quarterly, Caveat Lector, The Chattahoochee Review, Chicago Review, Chiron Review, The Classical Outlook, Coe Review, Confrontation, Context South, The Crab Orchard Review, Crucible, Cutbank, The Dalhousie Review (Canada), The Deronda Review, Dramatists Guild Quarterly, Dream International Quarterly, Envoi (UK), The Fiddlehead (Canada), Frank (France), Free Lunch, *The Great American Poetry Show* (anthology), Green River Review, Haight Ashbury Literary Review, The Hawaii Review, The Hiram Poetry Review, The Hollins Critic, Hot Metal Press, *In Whatever Houses We May Visit* (anthology), The Interpreter's House (UK), The Iowa Review, Isaac Asimov's Science Fiction Magazine, The Journal of Contemporary Anglo-Scandinavian Poetry (UK), The Journal of New Jersey Poets, The Kansas Quarterly, The Laurel Review, Light: A Quarterly of Light Verse, Long Island Quarterly, Lucid Rhythms, The Malahat Review (Canada), The Massachusetts Review, Midwest Poetry Review, The Milo Review, Naugatuck River Review, New Delta Review, New Letters, New Orleans Review, The New York Quarterly, North American Review, North Carolina Literary Review, Outposts (UK), The Outrider (Australia), The Palo Alto Review, Pembroke Magazine, Poet Lore, Poet: an International Monthly (India), Poetry Daily, Poetry Nippon (Japan), Poetry Salzburg Review (Austria), Poetry Super Highway, Princeton Arts Review, Prism International (Canada), Private Photo Review (Italy), Puerto Del Sol, Queen's Quarterly (Canada), The Raleigh News and Observer, Rattle, riverrun, The Santa Barbara Review, The Sewanee Review, Showcase '76, Sisyphus, The South Carolina Review, Southern Humanities Review, Southern Poetry Review, Spring: The Journal of the E.E. Cummings Society, Stand (UK), Tar River Poetry, The Tennessee Quarterly, Timber Creek Review, The Tulane Review, Verse, Verse Wisconsin, Virginia Quarterly Review, Voices International: an International Literary Quarterly, Voices Israel, War, Literature and the Arts, Wascana Review (Canada), The Webster Review, West Hills Review, Whiskey Island Magazine, The William and Mary Review, WordWrights Magazine, The Yale Review.

Penumbra: The space of partial illumination between the perfect shadow and the full light.
—*Johannes Kepler*

Penumbra: The "gray area where logic and principle falter..."
—*Justice Oliver Wendell Holmes, Jr.*

*for Patricia
my partner in time*

CONTENTS

First Season Alert xiii

PART ONE

Travelling Child 4
Come a Cropper 5
Paso Finos 7
The Letter, 1942 8
Camden, 1945 11
Case History 13
Impedimenta 14
Troop Transport 17
Tracers 18
Legal 20
Dry-Gulched 21
Carpooling it in the Caravan 22

PART TWO

Song: O Popular Moon 26
Chance 27
Aspects of Love 28
Carnival Sestina 30
Bereft 32
Above the High Beams 33
Not Forgotten 34
No Angel 35
Five Mile Movie Dance 36

Part Three

Singlewide	40
The Thin Disease	43
The Artesian Diver	45
Snowbound	47
Flashbacks	49
At a Classic Film Revival	50
Leadbelly	51
Destruction	53
Lipstick Skies	54
Roanoke Return	55
Swans at New Rochelle	58
Whistler	59
The Man Who Hated Cities	61
The Town Dump; or, Lily	63
New Man on the Docks	65
The Nun	67
Death and the Mermaid	69
The Diamond Merchant	71
A Worker at the Waterworks	73
Uranium Blues	74
Good Works are Love	77
Communion	78
To a Nightingale	78
The Islands of Langerhans	79
Family Tragedy	81
Scenario	82
Incognito	85
Gary Player Wins Masters	87
Ich Bin Drei Dinge	88
Lost Sketches by Bosch	89

Part Four

Lunacy	94
The Moon Tarzan	95
An American Poet on Tour	96
The Getaway	97
The Fallen Angel	98
A Tall One	100
The Ladies of Burdett	101
Two Sense Worth	102
Interview with the Diva	103
The Flight of the Vampire	104
Aquarius	105
News of 45	106
Scuba Eyes	107
At the Water-Cooler	108
The Delphic Oracle was a Pragmatist	109
Anarchus, Professor of English Lit	109
Oömancery	110
Van Gogh's Ear	111
Like the Titanic	112
Pedantic Piece	114
Goodbye Mister Bop	114
Classroom Rap	115
Monsieur Élan	116
An Honorary Mug	117
No	118
The Fruits of his Thought Delivered to his Favorite Bartender	120
The Last Word	121

Part Five

Ambitions	124
This Man Insisting Upon Living	125
Winter Waking	126
The Maestro and the Messenger	127
The Futurist	129
Life, A Western	130
Poetry	131
Houdini and the Dying Swan	132
Incident	135
On Wheels	136
Minim	137
Hush, Hush, New House in Charlotte	138
Allegorical Fountain	139
The Peruvian Apparition	140
A Reply	141
The Lesson	142
A Pile of Leaves	143
The Secret Agent	144
Spring and the Black Holes	145
It Must Have Been the Angels	146
Spring Rides	147
Bring Us a Ray	148
Walkie-Talkie	149
"Batter my Heart . . ."	150
The Loss	151
Morning Notes	152
See-Saw	154
Instant Angels	155
New Year Near the Hudson	156
Insect Song	157

Bad News 158
Trumpets of Doom 159
Dialogue of the Suicide and the Smoker 160
Brave New World 162
The Honey House 163
The Souls 165
Over the Magnolia 168
Because 169
The New 171

PART SIX

Commence Fire! 174
Old Icarus 176
Balding 177
Gin Rummies 178
Chronicle 180
Provenance of an Old Poet 181
Hire Actors! 183
The Nursing Home 184
Outside the Hospital 187
Those Who Die in Their Sleep 188
Now, the Fox! 189
Old Women, Pausing 190
Heart Failure 191
Death 193
Names of the Dead 194
A Memory 195
Emanation from the Penumbra 196
There I Am 197
Toward the End 198

FIRST SEASON ALERT

When I first woke   a child
how could I know   the spring rains

would take all summer   to rust
the autumn   how could I know

that flowers wilt   that trees
go bare   that birds fly away

that butterflies disappear
that green grass grays

that afterwards
the world could turn white

with dancing flakes   that, or
that it would all begin again?

PART ONE

TRAVELLING CHILD

Night: the rockety-rockety train:
the coach filled with sleepers: the moon
outside: the passing poles: by, by, by, by:
another child: friendship for a day,
for an hour like a lifetime:
a parting kiss at Kansas City:
Why? Why? I loved him. I loved her.
The khaki soldiers eating sandwiches:
candy butchers: Daddy? Hot. Cold.
Night and morning: death: time.

The magical furnished rooms, each new,
alive with new things to know:
closets that could be used for loneliness,
in which one might discover
the artifacts of a previous tenant,
or in which one might create
the lost cave, the bandit den, the jungle,
and, as each of these, the place
to crawl into: sanctuary.

COME A CROPPER

They head down
in a great slow motion,
as if they are galloping
into the underworld at some
suddenly found entrance,
with the amazed boy now
riding the underside of the huge,
stunned animal, like a ship's
captain on the belly of a ship
overturned and about to sink,
waiting for rescue, and nothing
heard but the horse's breath,
which struggled with the dry
hot air, and somewhere inside
that enormous exhausted body
the great heart finding its
rhythm once more.

Thrown
clear, the horrified boy
fans his horse with his hat,
crying, telling her he didn't
mean to hurt her, telling her
he loves her, begging her to rise
and be well, finally thinking of
the lake and water to throw on her.

Making his way to the lake, he
cannot imagine how in a half hour
she will rise out of her exhaustion

and plant her unsteady hooves
under her weight, and he
will lead her home,
along the shimmering,
dusty roads and among the cows
in the scrubgrassed fields of the
1940's dust bowl, limping, and frothy

on her flanks, like something from
the sea, home to her shady stable,
and to the master of the ranch,
to explain to such a man, how
he has galloped the legs from under
such a horse in the noonday sun.

PASO FINOS

Fine-paced, their manes sweeping the shortest
    grass,
their chins held in, like quick-stepping cadets,
almost miniature, they circle in wherever they are

like a carousel, and you can almost hear the music.
Sometimes they seem unreal, as if you watched
in a lucid dream the archetype of horse, the perfect

children's dream animal, the one that they could
    take between
finger and thumb and lift and place in air and see
the beautiful pinions form from barreled ribs,

and lean back giggling together as the little horses
    hover
and wing off, flying in the children's psychokinetic
imaginations, like Persian storybook animals, like

what should really be, and, amazingly, nearly is.

THE LETTER, 1942

His mother and father
could not understand
the extreme of his grief,
for his father's other
son was only half his brother,
and had not existed
in their lives but for letters
and occasional photographs
taken around the world
where the war was, often next
to his Wellington, or by
a field tent, wearing his wings,
a smiling twenty year old
whom he, the child in a yard,
thought must look the way
he himself would look at twenty,
and be a brave pilot
and take up the war
against Hitler and Tojo
in his turn, not knowing
that even wars do not last
forever. How could the child
be so devastated by the news,
who barely knew of his half
brother's existence? How
adults box things up
the child could not know
or believe. Hard rain.

Rivers of rain, as when
you look up through greenhouse

glass on a rainy day, crossed
his green eyes blotting out the blue
dry sky overhead, and
he told the rain of his grief and
he told the blurred, ugly yard
behind the city row house
with its junked, warped
furniture and strata of
ripped linoleum, roses
and geometry, and its wet,
stalking cat along the old spiked
wooden fence, run with rusted wire
meant to throw yourself on, told
the whole world, which was
all the rain of tears
out of his breathless,
heaving chest, narrow
as a chicken's, out
of his pounding seven year old
heart, and cowlicked hair,
that was trapped by the
four-sidedness of fence
and could not fly with his
grief as his brother the
pilot had flown, whom
he had never known.

Let the child race
pointlessly in

circles, trapped in the
square yard, and cry
himself out. The letter
was already over a year
old and smeared with
his father's few tears,
sad horrible history,
but must be set aside
so that life could go
on. "He'll get over it."
"I never thought—" said
his mother. "No, of course
not," said his father.
But the yard was sodden
with the child's grief,
whose head burned with hope
against fact that a mistake
had been made, that this fine
brother was yet to come to him
who had no one, whose
loneliness could not be
surmised by two wise parents,
kept sane by callousing death
and full of the hard world's rain.

CAMDEN, 1945

If I think of night, and factories, and day-bright streets,
   I get some of it. The whole town seemed to be a
     factory
full of graveyard- and swing-shifts and vox-populated
   streets
     at all hours, so that one lost track of night and day.

The children of Camden roamed the streets in gangs
   composed not so much of juvenile delinquents
as of orphaned children looking for something to do,
   their
     parents lost to them at Campbell's Soups or at Lionel
       Trains,

ground up in the Wheels of Industry. The schools
   didn't count,
     were apparently attended out of a need to get indoors
       for a time,
their schedules not fitting the schedules of the factories.
   Sleepers slept when they could, morning or evening

or night. Meals came when they did, now or later,
   morning or evening or night. I drank containered
     coffee,
ate stale chocolate donuts drizzling in wax paper, and
   huge greasy
     restaurant meat-cakes smothered in sour brown gravy.

In winter the snow was black, in summer the air was
   heavy.

   There was a constant grinding out of matter, of goods,
      of people,
but the funereal unreal light made one feel that no
   matter how much
      was made, the making was wages of sin, of death; and
      the whistles

blew and the sirens sounded and the mobs made their
   moans.
      The white faces were black and the black faces were
      white,
and everyone seemed to be slow-marching a treadmill
   to death,
      just after the war, once, in Camden, way back when.

CASE HISTORY

There was a time when no season prevailed,
when whatever season it presumed itself to be
held no distinction: day and night fell too
into the inconsequential: all units failed,
for they failed in the beholder, the keeper
of time: and all distinctions faded
between all things: for the beholder
could not distinguish one thing from another.
The curious will ask how this occurred.

This much we know: that there was love gone wrong,
and there was death, death of one most beloved
—all share the news—and there was inability
produced, nurtured, by the particular
way of the life itself: but even before
these triggers, fast and slow, were pulled,
the life had been filled with walls
within which lurked the known fear
and beyond which lurked the unknown fear.

And the child's head had been early cloaked
in a liripipe, shut about the eyes
as dark as blindness: and the mind,
in its strange bonehouse, dwelt, trying
to see into and through the dark.

IMPEDIMENTA

The rain flooded down the back steps and in under
the old linoleum, floating it, with its sad faded roses,
above the slab floor, an hallucination of a magic carpet,
the backyard's muddy effluvium oozing into every
    corner
and crevice and halfway down the hall to the bathroom,
and making my mother cry for all her hard waxing work.
My father, the superior drunk, had left us in this dump
in Newark to go off selling his bullshit books in
    Buffalo,
and to shack up with his beautiful vocabulary, quoth the
    raven,
a bottle and a bimbo, and not to have to sit here with us,
under the dripping pipes wrapped in soggy cardboard
by the puke-green wall of bricks with a thousand holes
in them for the bedbugs, roaches, and rumpled ringdings
that came out at night and crawled all over us, biting,
that swarmed like emigrating termites when the lights
    came on.
The asbestos-insulated furnace belched, farted, and
    hummed
outside our door, a jack-o'-lantern whose serrated teeth
did not scare the rats, who warmed to him, in his furry
    gray suit
that glowed in the dark, a giant rodent Golem. One
    could hear
him breathing through the thin walls that divided the
    superintendent's
apartment from the front basement, a pathed indoor
    junkyard.

We had to wend our way out through that La Brea Tar
    Pit
to get to the stairs that climbed and turned out to the
    street,
where we would peep up to see if anybody out there
would notice where we were coming from, which was
    out
from among the dented old metal cans full of raw
    garbage,
and what peculiar species of spelunker we were—what
Untouchables were surreptitiously seeking light and air.
I lied about my age and became a Western Union boy,
having shoeshined my way to the top, saved my money
and bought a bicycle, a Western Flyer, O Icarus! I
    found
my mother a pretty little apartment high over a pizza
    joint,
and we moved up into the air and the smell of baking
    dough.
My timid mother was shocked at such derring-do,
    daring
to fly so high, so near to the sun; and, for a while, we
    were
happy. But my father came home and said, "This place
    is too
expensive." We must get another sump-pump dump to
    superintend.
"Another nice basement that drips piss?" I asked, and
    added, "No,
I can afford to pay this rent, as I have been doing

for some time now. Now stick with me on this one,
Mom." *But we better do what your father thinks best,*
she whispered; and I said to myself—
                    "That's it, never again,"
as I helped to carry our embarrassing paltry posses-
   sions—
"Impedimenta" my father called them—through the
   streets.
My father led the way like a brass hat, soused and self-
important, my mother followed him into nothing but
   worse,
with a "Wither-thou-goest" and a last wistful look up
over the pizza parlor at our window of opportunity, a
dutiful wife of the Fifties, and I planned my escape.

TROOP TRANSPORT

We love to be hit by the spray
while watching the wake as the bow
dips five stories down and rises again
as if to take off for the clouds
where the gulls look down at us
as if we were sardines on toast
to snatch in their snooty hooked bills.
We love the sea, who knew only
the green rolling hills and cattle and horses:
but cowboys can't swim, so I stand
with my life-jacket on and stare
at the mountains of water and valleys
that keep changing places, loving the buck
and the crash of the bow and its wake
that sprays me with spindrift, mad
for its plunge full of colors, for
my face in the face of the moon-drawn,
gravitied deep. What ecstasy is,
is the danger of down, then returning,
like riding a bull till he drops.

TRACERS

Young, dreamy,
on a hill
dark as a
frown,
I fired
a fifty
-caliber
machine-gun
into the
night's abyss.
Every fifth
round
was a tracer
that flared
with a
wonderful
will as
it sought
the dark
ground.

What was
the magic
that night
that I could
never forget
how angelic
the tracers
looked,
losing their

light
without
whatever
regret
must be
humanly
brooked
when the
flare of
life flames
down and
into the
ground?

LEGAL

They stood in a cracked photograph before your tenth
birthday cake like puckered fountain cupids, helping you
to blow out your candles and in your wish. Your wish
then was that they would never grow old, a child's
wish, born of dependency, your need for them
to flourish for your sake. You looked away, about,
and wondered, if, upon your return to the mainland,
your parents would look the same as always, the same
as in the cracked photograph, or look old, altered.
You glanced up, and saw a long, black, tail-finned
limousine, shining moons of sun, pass out of
sight on the busy street where you entered the bar;
and, startled out of your reverie, you turned about
to find Waikiki Beach behind you, a keepsake
postcard of one of the most important days
of your life, and you wondered at the power
of your first legal drink to so disorient you;
for, when you entered, you were looking out at the sea.
Then you realized that you were on a turntable,
imperceptibly turning counterclockwise, but only,
of course, by the machinations of human will.

DRY-GULCHED

The mother-of-pearl
desert dawn
reddened. Grit-eyed,
I stared through
the Chuck Wagon's window
at an almost ghost
town of
haunted hotel,
false-fronted saloon,
hermitic mechanic's shop,
my Mercury lame,
waiting for
a new engine
with its block
not split
by Mojave heat,
and saw the celluloid
posse of
my matinee boyhood
ride in with the dawn.

CARPOOLING IT IN THE CARAVAN

a New York Transit Strike

Such amazement at reality
as to make it seem unreal,
and the knowledge of the
confluence of disparate events,
where impulsiveness and
inventiveness meet, such
amazement and such knowledge
have sometimes thrilled me
out of thought so that I
must seem a victim of logorrhea
in the library of life,
gleaning a joke out of the
quiet morning business commute,
the one the serious morning
newspaper readers want ejected
from the carpool.
Facts become treasures
in an uncertain world.
They are cheese to mice
on a flying mudball.
Since the past is deepest dark,
and no binding statement concerning
the future is possible, my fellow
travellers engross themselves
with the headlines and sports pages,
ignorant of ultimate purpose, and,
unlike me, content with now.

PART TWO

SONG: O POPULAR MOON!

—Moon Landing 1969

Now what kind of moon is it, darling,
    that, so blandly turning blue,
overhangs us here in greenly summer Brooklyn
    while the astronauts go round
and the sea at Coney rises,
    all its little lucky ripples
wiping off the darkened sand?

Now what kind of moon is this,
    questing for the old romance?
Acknowledging our loneliness,
    we know better than to ask,
returning from the Goldman Band
    and kinder songs of long ago.

Your pearl your blue your golden loneliness
    bring in our need,
which we acknowledge, seeing you
    sailing light, O, all unburdened.
Burdened by my loneliness,
    I hold her gentle hand in Prospect Park,
walking from the Goldman Band
    and the dismantling of the instruments.

CHANCE

For whatever reason,
we have found our lives
joined this morning,
as the sun roars up
beyond the patio and
its green vista.
You will have to go
beyond the chance
to find the purpose
of our being here,
like this, together,
beyond the purpose
once again to find
the chance. Rilke's
angels are the
potential others
of Planck's quanta.
Some seeds of time
will germinate,
some disintegrate,
and some, like us,
discover faces
in the mirror and
across the table.
I only know my eyes
see you (my neurons
say my eyes see you),
and seeing you I see
this moment as a
fragment of all love.

ASPECTS OF LOVE

*Three Poems in the Chinese Manner,
During the Cultural Revolution*

1. *OLD CHINESE COUPLE*

Their heads are touching:
one pillow in the middle of the night,
one dream from here to there
because they've been together so long.

In their dream,
they are meeting for the first time, again.
He remembers, she remembers, they remember.

Their arms are around each other.
They are warm together.
This is perfect.
But morning is near to mention
that everything is a revolution.

2. *A KISS OUTSIDE HER DOOR*

A kiss is two rumors:
her rumor of me in her,
and my rumor of me in her.

No, a kiss is three rumors:
the third rumor is of Yin or Yang,
the child. The rumor of a child.

It is the child in each of us
who is the rumor of me in her,
her rumor and my rumor.

A kiss is one rumor.
Listen to the neighbors talk.

3. REMEMBERING YOU

There is always more to remember.
Memory is like a mountain forest
inside my head—trees and trees,
leaves and leaves and leaves,
and there is always more to remember.
Now there is you, and everything about you.
And now there is that you are gone
and everything that has happened since.
Memory of you is like a new high mountain
and the trees are thick with leaves
and then all the leaves fall off
and the mountain sinks.

CARNIVAL SESTINA
A Tale of Love and Betrayal

Within the underbrush, beneath the leaves,
they sought the blinding sun for one quick flash.
The carny was in town, the crowd was quick,
merry-go-rounds were going round, and music
lent them its pace, though talk was near at hand
and certain someones wandered in the crowd.

When, later, they rejoined the noisy crowd,
she brushing from her skirt the golden leaves
that all that autumn fell, and he, his hand
above his eyes, avoiding the last flash
of evening sun, they noticed that the music
seemed in some doubt if they were dead or quick.

They separated then, and George was quick
to find the other two among the crowd,
who, when they saw him, laughed above the music,
crying, "You two were there, and then like leaves
in winter, gone! We lost you in a flash!"
"From this point on," said George, "I'll hold your
   hand."

"But where's my wife?" asked Keith. "I want *her*
   hand."
I haven't seen her, Keith," George lied, too quick
to answer, sounding false, and, in a flash,
it came to Keith that they had used the crowd,

his best friend and his wife, to lie in leaves,
betraying him and George's wife, while music

played, lulling them to think that love was music
like an unending song, and with a hand
drew George's wife to him, and into leaves
they vanished from the crowd, the others quick
to note that they were gone now from the crowd.
In leafy shadows, Keith told her in a flash

of his suspicions, also in a flash
what she had always hoped, and it was music
to George's wife, who hated that false crowd,
but truly loved dark Keith, who held her hand
in his and kissed it, slow, and not too quick-
ly drew her down with him into the leaves.

"We've lost them in a flash," Keith said, his hand
lifting her breast. "Quick now," she cried, "while music
drives on the crowd, and I wear only leaves . . ."

BEREFT

By artificial time, full of dates,
the pygmy time of people, not
the giant genuine time of stars,
she is late, the alarm rings out desire.
Artificial time is murdering his lust.
And the all-night lover of years ago
(his sleepy-eyed but vivacious wife
hurriedly hitching stockings to
garterbelt, slipping into heels)
looks on, bereft.
                  A hard life
has left him exhausted by night,
but a dream's sensual levitation
engages his tumescent morning lust.
Faithfully, this indiscipline of oversleep
by one who understands his plight,
he tries to see as healthy nerves;
although old men of the gold watch,
being doubtful of prowess, suspect
always a planned escape, yet
feign indifference.
                  The clock's
silent now, the old man blows smoke,
the coffee in his cup cold as his heart.
The choice was made between himself
and sleep. His wife had lust for sleep
and not himself. She has escaped
when she might have wakened early,
like a morning-glory, for his tested love.

ABOVE THE HIGH BEAMS

Parked
in the dark,
the motor running for
the heat against the winter,
with its packed and dirty snow
sinking in the soil beneath
the car, our divorce survived
by my loss of you, my youth,
by feelings that are hard,
and I've kicked out, hitting
the high beams, brightening
the bare trees, and spreading
a ghostly glow above them;
noticing how even that faint light
obscured the blinking stars,
the dulling and deformed
configurations of myth
punctuating storied night
with asterisks and commas,
exclamation points
and, o my lost one,
those damning, twisted
question marks. How
they decline, fade,
the longer I look
above the high beams,
the music of the battery-
charging motor making
an accompaniment
and a strangely endless

diminuendo to the late-
come light of the possibly,
but surely not surely, dead stars.

NOT FORGOTTEN

I went looking for the kisses
that I forgot to give you this year
and found them hiding in shame
behind a pile of silly arguments.

I gathered them tenderly in a basket
and put a red ribbon on them
and now offer them to you,
pretending they are roses.

NO ANGEL

for Patricia

Because you are you

& because they do not suffer
because their weather is never harsh
& they share nothing of the storms
that drive us in and burn us out
& because they are never in trouble
because they do not dance but on a pin
because they have no heat for anger
because they have no blood because
they do not eat drink nor defecate
& because they have no sense of humor
& because their lips are not discernable
but for a wide thin crease from ear to ear
& because their eyes are empty
but for the expansive light of heaven
& because they have not heard of sex
because they are never lonely
& because they do not judge
because they are not human
because they are abstract
& because their bodies are illusion
& because their wings beat nothing
& because they have no will but God's

you are higher than the angels

FIVE MILE MOVIE DANCE

You wore flowers,
something flowery,
and my arm around
your waist lifted
you, two, three,
maybe five miles,
dancing, never stopping
for the breath we
did not need, being
young, over all
obstacles, cars,
steps, up and down
porches, around fire
-hydrants and light
-poles, using them
like movie props,
swinging on them,
like a pair of
movie dancers,
Fred and Ginger, so
that we could remind
each other, all
these years later,
how we danced
through Brooklyn and
all the way home.

PART THREE

SINGLEWIDE

If they thought of us,
how all of us lived in the singlewide, fourteen feet
deep and forty long,
on no money but the wealth of God
sending us on our mission,
bringing seven children, his, mine, and ours,
with the early death he bore in him, to leave
me, after five hard, bleeding years,
rooms spattered with blood, aplastic
anemia hemorrhages, him, my love, gone,
and me left with the beloved brats,
the marina rich would know
it was their Christian duty to buy us out
at a decent price.

I tell the buyers how God told us
this was where to stop,
how I planted the redtips to shade the
thin back from the sun, the fig from the Bible;
how I lost my faith in sorrow at his death
and drank my way
into Alcoholics
Anonymous and found
my new man there, who pumps iron,
sweats tea, but wants beer,
a tattoo'd boy not older, not
less wild, than my son,
and needing a mother-wife,
why we drink iced tea in winter in this cold
singlewide, how he hauls red-necked dynamite to

mines on eight fat wheels;
and the well-dressed buyers look at me
like I'm crazy as I tell them
I'll sell real cheap,
but not as cheap as the
marina rich will pay
for a sad eyesore;
and they don't think I know investors
when I see them, who'll put some other
poor souls in here, or tear it down for
the lake land; crazy because I will take
the money to Texas on the border to start my dream,
my homeless and battered women's mission.

My big lug's trucker's license goes far. Only
a relapse to fear, to drugs or drink,
can stop my heart's compassionate work,
or the mission is mine, to bring them the
visions of Isaiah and the trials of Job,
which I know in my used woman's body,
burnt-up with sex and sin, my pretty nose
and cheeks fried with small veins
from the days of bleeding and empty death.

The buyers smile in kindness at my dream,
my mission, my need for direction—
they think they are too smart and can
live without God. Well, let them, if they can.
How much will they give me for my life? His anger
is not turned away and his hand is stretched out still.

I loved these woods that drop down to the rich man's
   lake,
condominiums, marinas, and the trees I planted to shade
my only wealth beside the Lord, my Savior.
But I bargain, with my stretch marks,
my unpainted, veined nose,
for my singlewide,
which no one wants, not even
these patient souls!

THE THIN DISEASE

Nearly seven feet tall, a skeleton
made of giant bird bones,
a bird-cage rib-cage,
his heart a little pulsing
robin, Kwame from Ghana
on the old Gold Coast
was my best friend.

Kwame had to reach down
to tap me on my red head. "Dutch,
we're going to cadge some drinks.
You do the talking.
Tell them I'm King Quazi
of oilrich offshore Quaziland,
and I can't speak English.
Tell them my kingdom is ten miles long
and a quarter mile wide, including beaches."

Kwame had purple-grey skin
and was so thin he looked like the shadow of a
    pole,
but his head was large and noble,
with cheekbones carved in slate,
and royally crested with a pompadour
befitting the son of a son of a king
from the ancient West African Empire,
though he was always church-mouse poor.

We worked on the New York docks,
off-loading ships, on-loading trucks.

He wasn't very strong. He drank a lot
and bled from the rectum when he worked.
They had to cut the grapes away.
Like a daddy longlegs and a flat red beetle,
we wobbled to a bar near St. Vincent's,
a knot of stitches still in his new tight ass.
He could ignore the pain for the booze.

He put his arm over my shoulder.
"Dutch, I'm going to die.
I've got the thin disease.
I'll never go back to Ghana."
"Sure you will. You'll go back."
There were good times yet.
But he died. He died.
He died. The white bed
was empty but for a wave-crested,
welted head, and limp hoses,
some of which were black
and leaked their fluids.
Ghana was far away, a dream,
but I was there, near, here,
his friend, holding his hand,
our funny different fingers
entwined, though pulling apart.

THE ARTESIAN DIVER

He pitched his diver,
a wine bottle half-filled
with water, into the air.
It smacked the lake,
and he pulled at the oars
until he came to the spot
where the diver had hit.
Yes, and there it was,
magnified to seem
just below the surface.
He watched the diver,
soon a mere fleck of light
indistinguishable from
countless others caught
by the sundrenched surface,
before they rayed down
and diminished in darkness.
The boat sank deeply on one side
with his over-leaning, his peering.
It floated gently sideways
through water that rippled
with the sound of tiny,
muffled bells. "He's through.
He can't take any more, either."
His elbow slipped off the side
and the boat rocked violently,
steadied. He scanned the shore.
All of them were waving at him,
smiling at him, and waving.
There was green-and-gold everywhere.

Even the water was gold.
He pulled hard at the oars,
the boat angled about,
and divided its wake
into two curved waves.
Then he saw his diver
rocket from the water,
high, shining, triumphant,
some distance ahead.

SNOWBOUND

How the free spirit suffers his winter out in the
woods is his business, isolated alone in an unused
farmhouse rented from a farmer by a tall strange city
man with a beard like a board & a wife who would
sleep in it but has left for the winter her husband
alone to be hermit at his request, an artist, poet &
painter, needing neither wife nor child nor sustenance
but vision only,

   that she go forth to the wicked city & fare there with a
former lover while he have visions during long mountain
downfall of flakes building to crescendo in white isolation,
that there be firewood alone was his matter, that chalk run
smooth over blackboard & vision come summoned by
white gods of sleet & snow & that that first time should
he die then the plan be known as faulted with no firewood
& the cold growing in his guts, that he understand what he
never understood, the seriousness of his state, & learn to
be a man once before claimed by the white tongue, snapped
like a spot from large blankness making no orientation:
be gone.

      He feared nothing but the thought of no vision,
      not the loss of his wife to another, nor the loss of
      his life, nor the meaning of loneliness, but for the
      vision forsaking all; was willing and willed that
      Death in a white coat with bony knuckles knock:
      his wife in wonder could not love her former
      lover but was young and thrilled at her husband's
      exploit, leaving the lover without chance as he

regaled her with delights on city nights of
restaurants and theaters for always she thought of
her strange visionary husband in the mountains
alone turning whiter and whiter like a snowbird
of some extraordinary kind with wings wide and
eaglehead highbeaked proud & coming down in
spring with great talons spread arresting her in
midflight at subway entrance & sweeping off up
up and away to his glee-echoing lair high on the
spiked cliffs—

    meanwhile the wise farmer who owned the house
had snowploughed his way to the visionary's door &
knocked like whitecoated Life & found artist frozen but
not dead, who awakened to strains of hospital music &
surrendered his soul to it, thanking the gods but not any
one in particular for the fact that only a few toes had
had to be removed—he liked his nurse, a warm vision
in white.

FLASHBACKS

You are doing something thoroughly mundane one day,
say, peeling carrots, and you are suddenly where
you once were while your hands go on with their work
and you are staring into the sun from under a shed
roof, where you and your other are arguing over
what you have done and now you remember that part,
the part of it that was about what you had done:
then you are wondering why you did it, what
ever possessed you to do such a stupid thing,
and it occurs to you as it has in a past you've
almost forgotten that you might have been arrested
for doing such a thing and no wonder that you and
your other argued over it, how could it have been
otherwise?
                    Of course it was a terrible mistake
to have made: it was a wonder that your other stayed
with you, who had done such a thing, but in the shed
in the last light of evening you finally made up and
even now you experience the sweetness of the kiss
of forgiveness as if it were warming your lips as you
peel the last of the carrots and you remember what
you are supposed to be doing though it is difficult
to draw away from that moment in the sunset shed
that seems somehow to be happening as you stand
where you are: but then you realize that you have cut
yourself and are bleeding. You must bandage your
   finger.
You must wash the carrots and cook them. You must
   not
forget this event, you think, as you have so many others.

AT A CLASSIC FILM REVIVAL

Walking down the darkened aisle, he stops,
shadows leaping about him. Behind the credits
rolling down the screen, the detective
hero strides a shabby street of cheap hotels.
I know that neighborhood. I know that boy.
Old Technicolor flashes in a static blizzard.
Still, he sees, or thinks he sees, *himself*
up there, behind the striding hero,
innocently tailing him, his own trench coat
collar up against the wet wind that was
blowing that day—for now he remembers
that day, but does not recall a camera
or a striding movie star ahead of him.
Someone shouts,
                    Sit down! Sit down!
He gropes the dark for a seat, dislodging others,
who spill popcorn and sticky drinks down on
his tissued pants and rundown shabby loafers
but keeps on looking up—at the image of himself!
—Oh so beautiful, that blooming boy!
He wants to be in Fred's Bar, to tell the flies
that he is in a film, or, at least, in the credits.
It doesn't matter that he got no credit, nor got paid.

LEADBELLY

for the musical ghost of Blind Lemon Jefferson

    Leadbelly, grim with your Cajun accordion,
with your harmonica blues, with your knife
    flicking down the twelve strings of your guitar
—the Rock Island Line was a mighty good road—
    bowing, scraping, white-suited trainman . . .
made your pride sick, but you sang,
    fast, strong, quiet, like a driven
demon, like you had to get it out
    before a razor dumped your guts
on a blood-mud taphouse floor,
    or some drunk crazy rednecks
nailed you up like Christ, in a dangerous world
    for anybody but most America for a black
poet of low-down places and sky-high loves.

    Leadbelly, thirty years hard time murder,
six and a half, sang your way out, ten more, intent,
    then Alan Lomax and his bro, John, folklorists—
makes you laugh inside at night—white boys,
    playing—but they get you out again and in
the Library of Congress, that grinding
    voice part now of something big, like
storm darkness, like that lifething,
    love, always beyond somewhere or
crying deep inside, in a dark place,
    yeah, big like music, big like that gal you
call Irene! How many Irenes, you think?

Even the Lomax bros, even them white boys,
they know Irene—you driving them through
   New York traffic, them folkloring in back and you
being their folkloring black chauffeur.
   You drink sharp liquor in Harlem, play
with Woody Guthrie, Sonny Terry, Brownie
   McGhee, the Headline Singers—radio too,
Hollywood and *Three Songs by Leadbelly*,
   a French tour . . . . You show 'em your razor
stretch marks, your shotpitted pot.
   Good night Irene I'll see you in my dreams . . .
all that good hot mean hard American life
   and Lou Gehrig's *amyotrophic lateral sclerosis*.
It's *The Midnight Special*!   Fade me, Death!

DESTRUCTION

In Florida a hurricane
came off the sea and
razed the town of
Homestead, in which
town lived a little
boy—in a mobile home,
a singlewide, on wheels—
whose hobby it was, he
told the reporter,
to build houses out of
cards. His mother worked,
his father had died, he
had no sister or brother,
no other, so when he came
home from school, second
grade, he would stack
cards, most beautifully,
the reporter gathered, up and up
and into the most wonderful
designs, so wonderful, he
said, that his mother
had photographed some of
his houses made of cards
(but the photos had been
blown away by the storm—
as well as everything else).
The boy said he could
stack some more, and
didn't care, his talent
remained, but frowned

and said, in a small voice,
that he felt sorry
for the wind.

LIPSTICK SKIES

She is Sunrise and Sunset, two women,
one who, in the morning, making up,
smears lipstick on her mouth, then sips
her tea or coffee, so that her smile,
while bright, is not quite tamed,
but somewhat wild against the morning sky
as if blossoming all over like a rose;
and another who has seen it all and lived
and still possesses quietly her passion,
which anyone can see, as she sinks down,
beyond her prime, beyond her day,
her sad mouth smiling knowingly
(for she has done some things she knows
that she should not have done,
has lived, has *lived!*) and now is near
the end. Behind the ridge her smile
breaks, with the lips of age,
crimson, plum, scarlet, not rose red,
for with the dusk she cannot see
to pick it out and put it right.
And she is thinking of a thing to say,
of some last word, as the great globe
raises its darkening horizon, but she
can only smile and kiss goodbye.

ROANOKE RETURN

Six-hundred miles above my southern exposure
my friend in extremis waits,
a man old enough to be my father,
and I am heading up North Carolina
in the long heartless dark,
to big, bad, only-the-dead-know Brooklyn,
headlights blazing on high beams,
being blinked at, warned and horned
—for I am faring to where one half
of my split spirit dies, in my war hero
drinking buddy, Elbert, two silver stars,
two purple hearts, smiling up ahead of me,
wan smile of age: Normandy's gone.

Tarheeled, tarwheeled, I wend my way,
blinking lights streaming into my brain,
to Brooklyn, that Elbert calls God's,
over hills of North Carolina night,
knowing the running greens and pines along the road,
how they set themselves against the running moon,
in my camouflaged combat jumpsuit
big enough for Santa jumping Claus,
soaked through with unholdable brew,
while the moon swings. . . the two moons
. . . and Elbert swings. . . in and out. . .
of the Fort Hamilton Veteran's Hospital
with his lungs smoked away, brave as ever—
Elbert, I give you a new medal,
the moon, the two moons, one for each
black lung—we will jag together once again

in your unbelieved-in-God's country,
where you might be looking at the moon, too.

It is a mad quest of hope and love
up 77 to Roanoke, link up with 85,
smooth overdrive to Harrisburg,
up the night to Jersey, climbing up,
up the great flying sky-harp cathedral Verrazano
and dumped at your Fort Hamilton feet—
Elbert, I salute you!

My olive-drab seabag bounces in back
like a wild love pregnant with burning vodka
and cheap-at-the-source Carolina cigs, deadly
gifts Elbert begged me to bring, only sooner,
in time for us to enjoy them together,
a lifetime of death brought now
and become magic to stop him from dying,
burning and unburnt offerings!
. . . in and out of smoking clouds,
lightnings, with the moon in and out,
escaping, seeking, avoiding love, age,
death, my wife, children, responsibilities
that begin in dreams. . . waves of water,
wind pressing me across lane lines,
and I am in the fast lane, pulling
around a slow-climbing eighteen-wheeler
honking like a tug, beaming me down,
wet speed and mild madness streaming away behind
   me.

It is a hot shower in a Roanoke motel room
and a nightmaring, dream-drunken sleep.
It is black coffee and a long-distance call,
and it is all too late, for me, for Elbert,
Officialdom now in charge of his skinny bones
—I hoped the metastasizing crab broke its teeth
on the embedded shrapnel that for fifty years
stabbed out through his skin in bloody stigmata
—and it is the long sad hungover journey home
in a day dark as night and relentless rain
falling down Virginia, North Carolina,
it is "Pardon me, boy. . ."
on the static-stuttering radio,
blanking, blanking out in the low country,
and it is the wrong rainy road, ascending. . .
looking out at water-colored what?
A Wailing Wall of water—
and I am high and outside, low and inside,
denim-backed white-duck fog and no lights, no cars,
no world but rain, alone, blood-shot eyes cotton-blind,
gearing up and down, burning brakes, clutch,
going round the side of something big
—the wet rockface of a Great Smoky,
with the steaming abyss of eternity below.
Elbert the Brave, be here as I quake,
strengthen me, breathless, on high,
going down, down down down too fast,
I dip, I spin, I slide, I am sideways,
backwards, tottering at a precipice
facing the past, rocking, rocking, stopped.

I am in heaven with nothing but down on one side,
hungover, scared—ALIVE—with the land down under
wet blue and green between layers of stranding smoke,
money in fog banks, and I pull off, away
from one possible end, sidestepping death.
All praise to Elbert, I am steady.
Love, I will be home tonight!

SWANS AT NEW ROCHELLE

I counted twenty-one swans
at the New Rochelle yacht
basin, while I sipped white wine.

Twenty-one! I thought of
Yeats, who counted nine-and-fifty
before he had well done.

But twenty-one swans is good
counting. So is one swan,
swans being swans and not

lesser creatures, like cars.
Twenty-one swans made me feel
proud, glad that I could count.

Often, I feel ashamed of it,
sitting in the window of a
corner cafeteria, counting.

WHISTLER

looked into his nocturne,
then up and down and side to side.
Which was the way? The water flowed
like a pale tongue from the horizon;
it grew wide and thick three-quarters up
the canvas, then dropped down the sides
three-quarters to a long thin tongue.
He could not resist the patch of land
in the close forewater two-thirds down,
or whatever floated there, nor the bottoming twig
that seemed to say he was a camera still,
though one instinctively out of focus.
But how not be a camera? Was it
unthinkable, the next natural step: to compose
with no more than patches, splotches of color?
Hugo had done it, but Hugo was a poet;
who would see his paintings? Who would care?
A pure abstraction? Whistler's instinct
may have urged him on, but life
warned not, and even so John Ruskin
called him coxcomb, said he flung
paint in the public's face—brush and pen
at war. Ruskin's world would not admit
a purely graphic language
of shape and color.

Nocturne in Black and Gold:
The Falling Rocket: how close
to spatter painting Pollock! How very close
to knowing how the essence is what counts!

True, Art won its farthing against Ruskin,
but the new vision remained unseen.
But had they asked how they could see,
those blind, Whistler might have said,
as he did to Oscar Wilde that night in the salon,
"You will, you will!"

THE MAN WHO HATED CITIES

moved to a small town
which rapidly became a city
and moved to a smaller town
which began to become
a bustling city
and moved out to the edge of town
but the edge grew populace
and nearly became another city
and moved farther out
to the edge of the edge
which immediately started to grow
and become another city
and moved even farther out
to the edge of the woods
which were quickly being developed
and moved into the woods
among the darkening trees
and saw some hunters
and moved back farther
into the deepest part
of the already over-
crowded woods
and finally found
a cave in the side
of a hill deep
in the darkest part
of the woods
and lit a fire
which cast his shadow
on the walls of the cave

in the hill in the
darkest, deepest
part of the woods
and put out the fire
because now he knew
that it wasn't cities
or towns or crowded
woods or shadowed caves
that he hated
it was people
even himself
his own
shadow

THE TOWN DUMP; OR, LILY

1880-1901

A Carolina Sinner

From the galling stones dumped down to fire
from the edge of the purifying fire and into it
starcrossed at night in the raging beams

from all things house from all things home
fried fish and olive oil and a halo of smoke
church bell cup and anchor cast from hearth

for him that John that love and lust was life
from town by galling stones and loving wives
by where the mill-freight siding runs with

bells and beams that light the night and halo the
    fire
Lily the lovely jealoused stoned and trampled
for the sun's sake inside her and her son

from her evil life in a small room to the edge
of town where a thousand shoes kick and fail
to shine but turn black and smoke like tar

that holds wings serpent and dragon of flight
for the loved Lily now bannered and pitched
sword ax lance and club Lily the peacock lamb

and dove Lily lion of love crowned king
though woman for the androgynous skull
and in her castration birthing the phoenix

her son rising from the burning feathers
for always flight at Kill Devil Hill
with angels and strangers upward in smoke

NEW MAN ON THE DOCKS

It's a pseudo-death, more or less. Your
whole system is paralyzed and you give
all the appearance of death.
                      —Working, *Studs Terkel*

The new men were issued key-chain badges
with numbers on them, then they were
divided into workgangs and marched off,
each gang to a different tractor-trailer truck,
to off-load its vegetable green-and-gold,
later to be loaded aboard the great gray ship
that walled out the harbor view like a dam.
The trucks had aluminum ladder-like rollers
placed from their side doors and resting atop
three or four stacked crates. Half the gang
lived down at the receiving end of the roller,
and the other half lived aboard the truck
and began shooting sixty-pound crates of cabbages
down at breakneck speed. He watched
the men ahead of him catch these whooshing,
wire-wrapped rectangular cannon-balls,
the bottom inside corner ramming
into their shoulders, sending them staggering
backwards, until it was his turn
and one of them was placed in position
to be fired at him. He heard a Samaritan
behind him say, "Don't catch it in the neck,
kid." He raised his shoulder and was glad
for his leather jacket when the concussion came.
He dragged the crate down from his shoulder,

then back, catching another crate, and off
and back in the line again. Soon the crates
were being fired at him with such speed
he fell into an hypnotic trance. He had no self
left, just a dream of whooshing crates,
chalk marks, and blurred, pained faces,
and didn't wake until he felt the planet
roll out of its orbit. The universe,
the quiet and beautiful music of the spheres,
was crashing. He stood waiting for the rhythmic
   thud,
and no thud came. He looked up. Everyone
was leaving him, shambling off without a word.
He wiped the fast-freezing sweat from his face
on the backs of his gloves. Then he shambled away,
   too,
through the dismal morning light of the waterfront,
by ancient, devastated buildings, dreaming of sleep.

THE NUN

I am looking at the bay
on the Staten Island ferry
watching the waves
crisscrossing each other
watching the wakes
of the wooden-shoe tugs
and the smoke
from their shoehorn stacks
catching Liberty
in the corner of my eye
but I notice the pretty young nun
as one notices a gull
or a cloud
I take in her youth
as I turn to the sea
of the bay
as one notes lovely things
and dismisses them
for they are not one's own
but belong to the church
or to the water or sky
or simply to life
I see nothing odd
but when I turn back
for the sun flashes
blinding me
I see the nun naked
her black habit down
at her small bare feet
her ebony hair flung wild

her blue eyes dancing
and she heaves by me
into the sea of the bay
into the afternoon harbor
like a white gull
or a cloud
against light
and then darker
blue or slate
rough slate
sharp slate
and the ferry turns
away from her
and I go to the other side
to see with others
where the nun went
and with relief see
her being pulled aboard
a police- or fire-boat
her slim beauty
lifted out of the water
wet and naked and
I feel somehow
finally itself

DEATH AND THE MERMAID

This mermaid is a virgin,
dreaming her last dream,
her upper half human and
milk-breasted, with seaweed-
tangled but human hair,
not an elderly patient
on display in a cave of plastic,
hearing the susurrus of the sea
in her own harsh breath.
She kicks, kicks open
her blanket-bandaged,
fish-tailed lower half
in her bound dream,
as the second tide
smacks hard on the rocks
a mile from the sanitarium
and foams in. *Life*, she cries,
in a siren sound, *life, life,*
under her plastic hood,
but Death dreams back
with a huge, curlicue wave
and spindrift, and the
cave-water rises, floating her up
on her forked, fish tail, where
she stands, breasts floating,
dark, tangled hair sparkling with
water-jewels, and leans forward,
into the tide, away
from a woman's world
of men, and reaches her

glistening long arms out
to take in the rising sea,
her only lover at the end.

THE DIAMOND MERCHANT

> *A diamond is forever.*
> —B. J. Kidd

The buoys of memory have faint bells, noticed in the
   night.
I have left these chiming seamarks for the time of my
   return.
They ring out there, but faintly, so faintly I can hardly
   hear.
I think they want me to remember the severances of the
   soul,
if soul is more than mere electric tissue. If Death is king
and I do not reclaim what I have jettisoned, it goes to
   him.
I do not want the king to have my life. Therefore, each
   night at sea,
I must set out to find the ringing buoys and haul aboard
the lagan realities, for now my aging body, my emotional
   mal de mer,
lend renewed reality to the cold, damp camps. One
   numbered friend
should wear a wedding ring, another was engaged, and
   yet a third,
below and silent, had eyes like Tavernier blue diamonds set
   in Fabergé
eggshell by the master. I cannot put a name to the
   smiling face I see,

but she existed, who is now the faint dream of a
   denouement.

    Shalom alekhem   *Shalom alekhem*

So now I sail all night to find them and their symbols, to
connect with them whatever seems appropriate, their
   rings,
their eyes, their ways: but not alone to find the persons
but to find the meanings of the persons to myself, the
   electric
mind, before the king should claim them from my life.

A WORKER AT THE WATERWORKS

He watched the water purling away.
No doubt it would soon be carrying off
loads of human excrement, with the lost
parts of bodies, dead cells, hairs,
bits and parts of burnt energy, the
stuff left over after the hard day's work,
after the argument, the loving in the
small bed while the kids slept fitfully.
There the tears of his beloved melted
into the blood, sweat, and tears of a city.

Off they go, he said, the domestic sewage,
and the storm runoff, to be wed and
to become the combined sewage; off it goes,
through flush tanks and scum collectors, through
grit chambers and sedimentation tanks,
through trickling filters and activated-
sludge units, through oxidation ponds
and the centrifuge, through heat coagulators
and into the incinerators, where, at last,
all our loves go up in smoke.

And the outfall works drop pure water,
cleansed, unsullied by any particle of humanity,
by any pitiful history of the human condition,
into the swaying receiving waters of river and sea.

URANIUM BLUES

Driveshaft

    distributing eighty, ninety, a hundred

  CLANG clank clank clank
outside Moab Utah
                          falling dusk
long white snake line
                      blacktop
shimmering off
                shimmer dimming out
mountains far
            low ahead
smoke a cigarette   wait   smoke

wait   sky bleeding up
down behind mountains   wait

sun's hiss   sidewinder's sandshuffle rattle
first long low leap of hare

car walls away last hot sticks of sun
cigarette's smoke-signal saves you
palm it & let it go   toot
toot
        a hum   something
down the road   crosseyed lights

stand up   wave   cowboy
like the cavalry   out & under
driveshaft down   pickup's got a tow
haul you in   patch you up   come daylight
get drunk tonight

            heigho Silver
gaining on   shadowed   etched
mountains   hauling ass   through pyramids
huge wide-based sinister cones   hundreds

through falling night   under stars
uranium
        inside mega-tons of pyramids
house up high there's Mister Big Bucks
made him a hill built him a house
them from Washington   big wigs
& queen bees
            down here's enlisted workers'
mobiles   hauled in   you ever
seen such a one?   long as a railway car
star-glitter's ore   hot stuff's in there
just awaitin' ta burn down hell   hot damn
we going to blow up the whole
freaking world
              break out the booze
we got us a writer here   going to Gollywood
play you a tune   strum strum strum
sing along   sing a song of uranium
uranium blues   glitter glitter

stars all over   up & down
same whole hotdamn universe
blowin' itself up   bee–you-tiffle
all night outside on the nailedtogether
radio active porch   strumming, swigging beer
on a tilting planet   singing the Big One
BIG ONE   everything doing a slow
burn   slow burn
                                        Heraclitean
rise up   up   Mister Sun
sleeping   until dark again   lit up

drive off singing   the atomic world
in the dark starbright early morning night
headlights glaring
                      singing Uranium Blues

GOOD WORKS ARE LOVE

Today I noticed, randomly,
on my shelf of poetry
Bill Empson and Bill Williams
sitting side by side,
the scholar and the doctor,
Seven Types of Ambiguity
and "No ideas but in things"
the intellectual and the
know-nothing natural man.

The war between what each
was representative of
is still alive, but why?
Each wrote poems one can—
admire? Each did his thing.

To think that in an art
requiring tolerance, at least,
a war abides between two ways
of working words for what they're worth
—it troubles, reminding us—
does it not?—of all intolerance,
of the religious wars, and of
the white-sheeted racist and
the hanging black-skinned man.

COMMUNION

I lie in the darkness and listen into silence
sometimes, outside the stream of time
where life hums and burns with its moths and flames,
its mechanical tropisms of desire and death;
I listen to the silent voice of the nightingale
with my friend Keats, the dead boy, the poet.

TO A NIGHTINGALE

Lifting your lamp
in dark Scutari, where
the wounded could see you
plunging amidst their cramped cots,
they honored you and
you changed forever the way
wounded were cared for.

What makes an eminent Victorian?
Merciful gifts from your pocket
when England refused to expend
on working-class wounded,
the blood-giving soldiers
of Queen and Country.

THE ISLANDS OF LANGERHANS

Islands of Langerhans—
scattered cell groups in the
pancreas which produce insulin

Stream of consciousness, WWII Veteran,
Hospitalized, diabetic, dying...

in memory of an uncle

<pre>
         Woke once to   ukulele music
     white-smocked aliens   on the crystaline
         their poetic rap   Islands of Langerhans
             the crystaline   emerald islands
        active principle of   in a crystaline sea
    the Islands of Langerhans   in Oceanside in
                     insulin   Golden Land
          palm trees swaying   Silver Hollows
              ukulele music   in Golden Land
                    sarongs   near the sea
      Hollywood presents the   where you can see
        Islands of Langerhans   the Islands of Langerhans
             with Boris Karloff   in an echo
               as Langerhans   of crystaline footsteps
     the mad scientist who   down a hollow hall
                     invites   where white-smocked aliens
 the alien pod people to land   rap poetically
    and institutional footsteps   where you forgot to take
          down the hollow hall   your insulin
      hollow footsteps down   you know you can go
             hollow footsteps   into sugar shock or
           in an echo chamber   insulin shock
   Silver Hollows near the sea   if you don't take care of
</pre>

                    your only friend   at the neck
                  and you like a kid   and drove down
                  have to spend all day   and out through the ribs
                         at Disneyland   under the right arm
                  eating cake and candy   rapping he'll be out of it
                      and swilling beer   in a day or two
                            unbalanced   rebalance of sugar-insulin
Disneyland in Golden Land   treat as shock
                             Hollywood   then nothing but
                               sarongs   the white-smocked aliens
                         ukulele music   who landed at Langerhans
                     palm trees swaying   I was afraid
         the Islands of Langerhans   when I saw them
                        their crystaline they echo'd and echo'd
                       active principle   down the long hallways
                      poetic rap of the   a Silver Hollows sound
                  white-smocked aliens   but they will transfer me
                      who took samples   to a VA hospital
                        of your blood   heard their crystaline
                   on a raised white table poetic rap
                                          footsteps
                                          echoing down
         The beach at Langerhans   wasn't afraid of God's
               is heavily fortified   musical castle
          and there's a rough surf   wasn't afraid at all
                          many died   because old was young
          before they hit the beach   when we hit the beach
          awarded the Purple Elvis   at Langerhans at
                and the Flying Saucer   not Langerhans
          for the bullet plugged in   at Normandy

FAMILY TRAGEDY

> *Show me a hero and I will*
> *write you a tragedy.*
>   —F. Scott Fitzgerald

    Sweetheart of somebody else? It was Joy, she
cried, and your children were listening. Joy, she cried
        out, and again, Joy, she

    screamed, as you strangled her there, as the children
watched you in horror. It must be erased!
        They must never remember!

    Killing my cousins was hard, you said, hard. They
broke your crazed heart, because they'd never
        feared you. They went with you then, and

    breathed in the gas. Was it fear, or was trust there?
Children my age! Then you poured gasoline
        in the house and set it on

    fire. I was back from the service myself, when,
urged by my father, I visited you
        in your bedlamite world, a

    deathless and tortured thing, uncle. I winced at
sight of your burnt-paper face, and your
        fingerless hands, and your hair, so

    strange in its pattern. I'd seen you before, but
then, to a child, you seemed silver and gold,
        home from hell, and a hero.

SCENARIO

There was a young priest
who stalked the pornographic
night of the X-rated
movie houses and the
prostituting streets
outside them in what had
become a sexual compulsion.
Sometimes he felt that he had lost
all control of himself and
with that loss his very soul.
But his soul was saved through
the confession of his sins
and their forgiveness
by a fellow priest who
was not his own publicly
acknowledged confessor
but a fellow sinner,
an older priest who had had
a twenty-year quasi-marriage
and who would in turn ask
the young priest for
absolution after
confessing to him. When
the young priest made
confession to his acknowledged
confessor and spiritual guide
a little later, he had only
to confess to the evil
thoughts of the days since
he last stalked the streets,

thereby keeping his
spiritual guide in the dark.
He behaves as if in a
dream when he is in the grip
of this compulsion, as if
he himself has become a
character in the dirty
movie he is watching,
and in this state of
disassociation picks up
the first prostitute he sees,
and, with release, becomes
guilt-ridden and disgraced
until he must seek out
his secret-confessor.
He will find a telephone
within minutes of the event,
plug in the number, wait,
and say in a voice
thick with mixed emotions
of shame and anger,
"I must see you."
His secret confessor
never refuses,
no priest does,
but he will take
the confession with a
heavy heart, for
his friend and
for himself. The

confession, it seems,
has become part of
the compulsion, as both
have come to suspect.
Advice is traded,
elements of which might
have proven helpful to
either priest, but none
has been acted on,
until . . .

INCOGNITO

Le monde est le livre des femmes.
                    —Rousseau

Imagine arriving, ermine-clad,
thinking yourself forgotten there,
in a village in a valley, nearly a col,
ringed by alps, in one of those mysterious little
border countries in the Balkans, having chugged
uphill and tobogganed down until
you have left the other world behind,
where it is real and true, and have come finally
to your Ultima Thule, a guttural in a tongue
nobody outside knows; where,
stepping down from the powerful, steaming
train, containing the last of the known world,
you become again part of the place where you began,
unknown and young and beautiful and frightened,
decades and decades ago, before the shame and scorn.

Thanks to the enormous wealth you have amassed
as a world-famous courtesan, you have kept
your health and strength—money for monkey
glands, spas, etc.—and with them
some of the qualities you had
as a youth, particularly your fierce,
imperious temperament. And everyone moves at
the tilt of your wide-brimmed hat, everyone bows
—for even here there has been news of you—everyone
looks up at you in awe—your great height an
illusion created by power—and you say, finally,
after a lifetime of waiting: Bring them to me,

those who so hurt me that I had no choice but to
   succeed.

Your beautiful rival of youth waddles up.
She is just your age, but looks a thousand,
horrible, hairy. You sicken at the sight,
this porcine hirsute sight. She stole your man.
He stands beside her. What, not him! You give them
   alms.
But what of the dreadful mayor? Dead, long dead.
And what of your former employer, that hateful
   woman?
In a nursing home, gone daft with age. She sometimes
calls for you. They sweep you off to see her.
And she calls for you. You bring the bedpan in
yourself. You pat her hair. Where have you been,
you dreadful girl? You've been around the world
in company with kings. The *Almanach de Gotha*
mentions you. When your mistress falls into a
   comatose
dementia, a talking, tossing sleep, you watch the moon
sail across her curving window, and make a mental list.
Surely somewhere there is someone worthy of your
   wrath.

GARY PLAYER WINS MASTERS

Poetry is news
that stays news.
          —Ezra Pound

"The beloved draws the lover," Aristotle says.
We are wanted to be what we become.
Chester Carlson, inventor of
xerography, died in 1968.
Think of it under the stars.
Or think of this: "Greek Fire,"
a missile weapon of sulfur,
rock salt, resin, and petroleum,
was invented by Kallinikos of Byzantium,
in 671. He shall not be forgotten.
Poetry is an accidental of essence.
It could have been drumming,
had I been able to afford a drum.
I could always come up with a piece of paper
and a pencil. In 1788 James Hutton wrote
a "New Theory of the Earth" and Laplace
came out with his "Laws of the Planetary System."
(Also first hortensia and fuchsia imported from Peru.)
Aristotle says, "Essence is the principle of every
     thing."
It's the unchangable that makes change possible.
Substance is what we stand under.
Becoming is guided in terms of a goal.
"Greek Fire" turned atomic.
How do we calculate the goal? What should
poetry turn into? Does a new century require
a new kind of poetry? Has the Information Age

created it? 1961: Jack Nicklaus wins U.S. Golf
Association Amateur; Gene Littler
wins Open; Gary Player wins Masters.

ICH BIN DREI DINGE

I

Ich bin drei dinge.
Natürlich, ich bin ein Mann;
aber das ist nicht viel.
Es wäre etwas.
Es wäre ein Anfang;
aber es ist ein Ende.
Sie können aber sagen:
Ach, 's ist doch nur ein Mensch.

II

Und ich bin ein Arbeiter
doch keiner Bemerkt meine Arbeit.

III

Und drei: der Tod treibt herum
wie ein wahnsinniger Vogel,
und ich bin der goldne Kern.

LOST SKETCHES BY BOSCH

Is it true that they have been found in a bedpost,
the most profound and diabolical of Bosch's visions,
such recisions of budding life, such deracinations,

that the curators will only allow medical-psychological
bureaucrats and high government officials to see them?
Is it true that a journalist who moled his way into the

museum was hysterically blinded; and that psychologists
warn that the health of the public must be protected
from the homunculi of Hieronymus Bosch? They
   wondered:

Were his works the result of an old painter's colic?
Did he hear in the braying of an ass the voice of a man,
praying? Was his large breakfast egg humanly
   impregnated

to form such a melancholy yolk? Young Hieronymus
   saw,
his mother used to say, through the holy mask of
   benevolence.
She told how he could sense what was there, and tell her

the hell beneath the inevitable illusions, the true tree
spring-budding grinning grotesques wearing black
   wreaths
of dried blood. Some say he had access to alchemists'
   jars,

because the imagination must base its visions in fact.
It's evident now, they say, in light of these gory graphics,
that he had to tone down, make less consequential,

his best-known paintings to make them at all acceptable.
O, that his mother had burned and not saved out of love
these abominable sketches by the young Hieronymus
   Bosch!

PART FOUR

LUNACY

I
can't
wait for
two more
weeks if I
take it now
if I ate it now
I'd have got only
the half of it but
half is better than
nothing & I need my
fix of the moon. I
open the window &
reach for the moon-
pill & pull it down
& push it in & chew
the moist cheese of
it in the green cheese
of it & begin to
feel the effect
of the dog's moon
the wolf's moon
& chew & swallow
& swallow &
chew grinding
& swallow
& finally
*HOWL
!*

THE MOON TARZAN

Have you seen the moon
Tarzan swing through the trees
at night? Some people I know
like to say it is only the moon
and the shadows of trees,
but I have caught it
in the interstices of the trees,
a silver Tarzan swinging along
at an unbelieveable pace,
flashing hand over hand,
feet trailing down
through the shadows, flickering,
with a chimp on his back,
and a twinkling Jane
hanging onto his foot. Boy Mars,
Jane the evening star, Cheetah
on his back the moon's glow,
and they swing by so quickly,
only what's left of a child
can see them. An elephant's
yodel cracks the rustling quiet
of the night, down by the tracks.

AN AMERICAN POET ON TOUR

I suppose it was somewhat
like this in the Hellenistic
age, when you could go in every direction
from Athens and still be a Greek
and I suppose it was somewhat
like this in the Roman
when all roads led away
and back to Rome and
I suppose it was somewhat
like this when the sun never set
on the old British Empire,
so this is what we Americans get
for being the so-called superpower.

I have been thinking these thoughts
on a plane for an hour—
how every place I land
seems like the place I just left—
and now I think I understand
just what Gertrude Stein meant
when she said what she said
in her odd and idiosyncratic bent
about the place she had come from
where there was no there there.
Anyway this morning wherever I am
the weather seems fair
and I'm sure to like it there.

THE GETAWAY

There was a rosy dawn in the mountains,
but it was the city he needed;
there were morning stars; but he needed the rain-wet
ashcans and the morning Danish.
He needed the containered coffee and the dank puddled
　　streets
and the steam up like a seeping vapor out of hell
from the drains and the hellbent crowds
walking right over the tops of taxis
in the impossible pace; he needed
the banana-peeled gutters and the knife in the back
and the long low slow limos with ominous dark
　　windows.

There was a rosy dawn in the mountains
and there were early morning stars and a scimitar moon
and the cabin hung over the cliff and groaned
and the rainbow trout would jump right into your net
and you could breakfast on trout every morning
and while you ate the sun would run along the cliff
and turn everything into gold.
You could write all morning to the warbling
in an ornithologist's dream; but he needed
the poem of the city in order to write of his hero,
the gumshoe, the poor sucker the city folks loved.

THE FALLEN ANGEL

Angels have never been people,
so coming down to Earth was a pleasant surprise.
He landed on a river boat in Mississippi, heading north,
wearing a wonderful gray suit
with a waistcoat, and a tall gray hat,
his pockets full of Dix-notes.
He liked himself so much
he forgot what he was there for:
something to do with changing the future, he thought.
But, right now, well, he was too excited to think about
    that,
too filled with what must be human sensation.

He was on deck, and the river was foggy,
but he could see the bank, and a sign: Natchez.
The bank was filled with clouds of waving greenery.
From somewhere on board a band's gay
tunes rose in the air.
He began to beat time on the deck with his foot:
a real foot—and no wings!
He tipped his hat to the passing ladies,
who nodded from behind fans.
Some of the men frowned at him.
Were they jealous? Of him? He was joyous!
He gambled and won, gambled and lost,
gambled and won again.
The night in the saloon
was the most wonderful night of his existence.

He slept with a woman that night. She robbed him and
got lost in Natchez. He didn't mind.
No, not at all. It had been exhilarating!
He gambled again, cheated, and someone shot him.
He died and became a ghost.
He liked being a ghost much more than he ever had
   liked
being an angel. Now he had something to remember,
having forgotten why he had been sent down
as an angel in the first, blessed place.

A TALL ONE

*Years ago, McSorley's Old Ale House
in New York City refused to serve women.*

I, too,
wasted my time
in McSorley's
smokey Old Ale House
with no women
but once
sneaked a tall one
in wearing
a slouch hat
with her hair
stuffed under
in time to find
a combat zone
where a famous
British act-
OR had been
snug in steamy
old McSorley's
but, tables turned,
the bartender
in a sweat drawing
a round—
"Trevor was here
and had a fit"—
my tall friend
giggling like
a little girl

           (he gave her
          a doubtful look,
           but served her
            a Stout). My
            elbow in her
              slim ribs—
            her new deep
          voice, "Thanks!
            and cheers!"

THE LADIES OF BURDETT

The ladies of Burdett
are straight tall wonders
as they think on men . . . .

Beside the country road
the grapes are plump,
the plums weigh down the springing boughs.

When Benjamin Franklin
invented bifocals
it was for the ladies of Burdett.

But this does not mean
that these wingless angels
of the consequential

do not, at midnight,
have bright red dreams
that give tone to their cheeks.

TWO SENSE WORTH

PRETTY

as a black
rose
the sleek
little black
snake
rode the
broom handle
to the grass
& vanished
in it
quickly

A BUSYBODY

a busy
body be
comes an ac
tivist be
comes a ter
rorist be
comes my
way or high
way or
die

INTERVIEW WITH THE DIVA

Diva, you rise to a day you have worked for so long.
Are you proud now? "Proud? There is pride and then
   pride.
Washing my face in the suds of the morning,
      I glow for the day, tra la la!"

Your singing voice seems a voice out of time, out of
   space.
Is it God's voice? "No, voices of sisters from time
echoing down, contralto, soprano, singing love,
      singing loss, tra la la!"

Any last word, on this premiere morning, with the birds
singing so sweetly? "On mornings like this one should
   sing,
sing with the birds in their green opera house,
      comedy, tragedy, tra la la!"

THE FLIGHT OF THE VAMPIRE

The poetry of the vampire
is not in its bloodlust,
nor in its daylight
coffin-kept comas,
but in its nocturnal flights
under the moon. Think
of the beauty
of those flights, the new freedom
felt, the anticipation
of direction, the beating
back of fresh air. Once
in flight, the vampire fears
no stakes in the heart,
no sun on the neck, no
empty mirrors, but
between the poles
of its evil life
of the undead
can enjoy the freshness
of the wind, the sparkle of stars,
the big face of the man
in the moon, the close
swishing of wings
made by the winged
creatures of nature, and
almost know again, if ever,
what it is to belong
to life, not death. It is
at this time that all vampires
are at their best,

their mouths shut
in a tight smile
for the breeze,
their dead eyes,
impossibly,
almost laughing.

AQUARIUS

We dreamed the Golden Age
we wanted you to be,
our long hair hanging loose
and blowing in the wind,
our beads, our sandals,
jingling, flapping on our
feet, our feet encrusted
with good mud, smoking a
joint, and nodding, word-
less, for it seemed we had
no words with which to
get beyond the chaos of the
conscience back in that time
of undeclared and endless war,
and back to Batman, Robin,
and the Joker's gang, where
Good was understandable,
for not at all complex,
and Evil slunk away,
its lesson learned.

NEWS OF 45

Into his mid-life crisis
desperate man stalks wild
life brings home head of
thought for wall display
mounting it for worship
plenty yet more to come
proudly shows it to friends
who scoff saying some
body else got it for you
like hell they did shot
gun see all the holes
in it but its mine mine
mine proud of it autumnal
macho laughable necessary
joy so worry not thy heart
days of glory upon thy
wrinkled brow sparks
of plenty more to come
next better yet which
could be worse who
knows but plunge on
plunge on with no effort
for light takes you
smilingly home as you
stay & practice your
declensions sun-o
moon-a your conju
gations selvesyes
selvesalways selves
before selvesafter

glory glory glory
for my five & forty.

SCUBA EYES

They travelled on a wave,
looking up and down and around,
like drifting jelly fish.

They rolled on the wave's crest
and scudded toward the shore
in a valley of green water.

They saw that the day had lightened,
and that others strolled the beach
for the sunrise on the sea.

They saw seabirds in the sky,
and, just below the surface,
the fish that were their prey.

They focussed the beach and the town,
the pavilion and the steeple,
as they rose out of the surf.

They looked back at the tossing sea
from a face without a mask
and felt its brisking breeze.

They finally followed the others
in their promenade along the strand,
watering in the sun.

AT THE WATER-COOLER

Outside, a taxi honked
and the traffic lurched
to green. I considered
such methods as I knew:
the vacation in Bermuda,
the slopes of Aspen,
Waikiki. As the sky
drew down its curtain
toward five, I thought
of him again, the
heart-broken, the hard
glass of his heart
in shards and
cutting his entrails;
yet, as if by magic,
holding his red
blood perfused with
luncheon port. I had a
tiny spot of red on my
pale yellow shirt.
His wife could not
commiserate, as he
had thought me able
to, for his lost mistress
of the water-cooler.

THE DELPHIC ORACLE WAS A PRAGMATIST

Those in charge
of its steam-engine
gates to the future
compared notes

on the past. To be
on the safe side,
their prophecies
were cryptic.

They threw parties
after a good prophecy,
and all their jokes
were about the great.

ANARCHUS, PROFESSOR OF ENGLISH LIT

I am Anarchus, King of Academe,
tenured to bring chaos to your campus.
I can say any goddam irresponsible fucking thing.
I am a regular irrepressible intellectual Wild Bull of
   the Pampas.

OÖMANCERY

Oömancery is the magic of the universe
popping out of an egg.
I don't see why the universe should not
pop out of an egg, or into one.

I read with my morning coffee,
in the *New York Times,*
of a new theory of physics,
providing for the possible

existence of multiple universes,
unknown to one another.
I don't see why there should not be
multiple universes.

I am so intrigued by the notion
that I fail to notice
that there are innumerable presences
in my house and that they are

attempting to tell me something.
I catch myself up and listen
but can only hear suggestions:
Mister Breeze, Mistress Boardcreak,

Master Bark, and little Miss Sigh,
speaking ineffably to me. Zounds!
Are their voices coming from my holy egg?
The light on the walls is

filled with dancing wings.
My egg is beautiful,
but not too beautiful to eat.
I swallow the soft-boiled universe

whole, and wash it down with coffee.
Now I am in one and have one in me.
The theory of multiple universes
has been proven to my satisfaction.

VAN GOGH'S EAR

I have no friends
how can I have friends
I only know artists
arrogant egotistical
disagreeable people
like myself, so how
in the name of Van
Gogh's ear am I
supposed to have
any friends?

LIKE THE TITANIC

Earth was to warm, the icecaps melt, and the land disappear
in a large low sea where the continents would rise like tropical islands
beckoning the water-stranded, the arked, the rafted and the routed,
but instead Earth cracked in two, making commuters work harder,
and instead of a Nuclear Winter there was the Radiant Summer
and instead of the Third World War there was the Time of the Thousand Fracases
and the last pair of African elephants was saved by the Cartel of Poachers
to be bred for their ivory which at long last was discovered to
actually have medicinal value and aphrodisiacal effect,
and everyone learned Turkish, making the Common Market an unanticipated success,
and there really was a Man in the Moon, which turned out to be a well-disguised alien listening post
and the point of origin for flying saucers, which the KGB and the CIA,
who had been working together for years, had known all along.

No, the meek never did inherit Earth; instead they grew cruel and

powerful and took control from the rich who had grown
   kind
and Halley's Comet returned twice in one year,
confounding astronomers, who now project that it does
   this every millionth turn,
but where it goes when it does this nobody knows
even though many are prepared to stake the world on
   their theories,
speaking of which, Einstein and Planck never could be
   reconciled
and instead of the poet dying like a young swan an old
   one honked on monotonously
into the night, only saving his audience with much cheese
   and wine,
once again proving himself in error, according to human
   certitude,
which any fool can prophesy, is not to be trusted.

PEDANTIC PIECE

If you have no verbs,
you must *do* everything;
but, really, you must not:
not, for instance, *do* dope.

May I lend you a verb?
Do you wish to *use,
misuse, abuse,* to
inhale, inject, ingest,
or do you wish to *do,* dope?

Well, don't; don't *do* dope.
Do do something else.

GOODBYE MISTER BOP

When Chips left the Old School he wore its tie
and was carried out with his Wellingtons on.
But no way Mister Bop, the Burnt-Out Prof.
Things definitely ain't what they used to be.
Bop gets to retire on something like a 401(k);
but not yet, as St. Augustine put it, not quite yet;
I'm not ready for retired sainthood yet!
The syllogisms from which Aristotle deduced the valid
are not complete. In American institutions
we fail upward to glory, and I expect
to be the mad head of the English Department before
I wallop my last tennis ball to cardiac arrest,
or do my last imitation of Johnny Weissmuller.
"Thanatopsis" is *not* my favorite poem.

CLASSROOM RAP

"Coleridge did dope," she said.
"So one day, when he was socked out,
dreaming up this poem about Xanadu,
along came this person from Porlock
on some business and shook him out of it.
After about an hour he couldn't remember
anything but the first part of the poem.
Has that ever happened to you? I mean,
that poem of yours in the 'American Scholar'
seems unfinished, you know?" A very
finished young lady, and this is what
I get! I give them some *Biographia
Literaria*, in a vague hope . . .
"Fancy and imagination!" I roar,
and point to someone else.
"Fancy is only memory and produces
only a sensational product.
Imagination transcends time and
makes contact with higher reality."
Something occurs to me: "No,
I don't *do* dope, and the poem
is finished because it says
what it started out to say
in the way it started out to say it."
"I only meant, have you ever been
interrupted when you were writing
a poem, so that the unfinished part
transcends and makes contact with
a higher reality, like that one
in the 'American Scholar'?"

And suddenly I realized how very quick
she was, and nice, and pretty too.

MONSIEUR ÉLAN

He insisted on life before death.
He went about waking people up,
refusing to let them sleep,
shouting "Rise and shine!"
He played a bugle call.
He was all for the sun.
Everyone began to hate him
and to shun him.
But he sought them out,
banging a tin drum,
commanding quick march.
He pursued them through life
like the spirit of life,
glad to be trouble.
Finally, finally, finally,
we attended his funeral
and went home to bed,
just dead.

THE HONORARY MUG

Note: MUG: a degree awarded by the School of Hard Knocks, Newark, N.J., where it stands for Most Ugly Guy.

> *Poetry is a mug's game.*
> *—T.S. Eliot*

Pretium affectionis
is set upon my pin,
because I'm like the others
in my desire to win
for old Hard Knocks what glory
I can upon the field
of action in the story
"Knockians Never Yield!"

Once in its jocund halls
where poison ivy climbs,
"Knockians Know Best!"
will ring like rusty chimes.
And when they pass the hat
for an endowment buck,
H.K. alums will vanish,
for they have all the luck.

Oh I can't wait to get there,
with Gattling, Gunn, and Thugg
(and Preacher Crook!), to get
my honorary MUG!

NO

The world says No.
It has a genius for No.
Everything is No.
In the beginning was Yes
but the world says No.
By the world I mean the people.
The people No.
The people say No.
Authority says No.
Power says Yes to itself
but No to everyone else: it says No.
The police say No.
Sometimes, assuredly,
it is necessary to say No.
But I say No,
it is not always necessary to say No.
When the new child wishes
someone always says No.
When the dog barks
at his own wagging tail,
someone says No.
When the cat runs sideways,
his back up, playing,
someone says No,
you'll break the lamp.
The world says No.
When someone has a new idea,
the world says No.
The world likes to say No.
No means I know better.

No means I am stronger.
No means I am Yes and No.
The world says No.
The people say No.
Authority says No.
Power says No.
The police say No.
The teacher says No.
Love might even say No.
No is the genius of the world.

THE FRUITS OF HIS THOUGHT DELIVERED TO HIS FAVORITE BARTENDER

The good man is like
the camel, George,
he standeth humped!
Drink not of the milk
of human kindness,
for it is binding!

Once a ladyfriend
tried to shut me up:
"Stop sounding like
a garrulous guru!"
she shouted.
"Be yourself!"
But then she thought,
and then she said,
"Oh, hell, you *are*
being yourself!"

She was looking
at *her*self in a
beautiful mirror,
and spoiling it.
"Art thou ugly?" I said.
"Not in the eye of the needle!"

THE LAST WORD

Edwin Makepeace Thackery Schorb
wrote many words into his books,
drank too much beer, and lost his looks,
and then spun off this spinning orb.

We who knew him say that he
was quite mistaken in all he did;
others, however, from whom he hid,
called him a genius, readily!

What is the truth? Oh who may know?
Not I, who knew him when he was young!
Nor I, who wagged a flattering tongue!
Say this: He drank, and had to go!

PART FIVE

AMBITIONS

I would like to write a prologue to all that is noble.
I would like to ratify and validate the good.
I would like to express a few cogent thoughts
with regard to love.
I would like to express myself in terms of flowers.
I would like to tell you all about squareness
and a little at least, about weight.
I would like to remind you
that the blood of wood
can look like
the disintegrating
arrangements of roses
when observed from the corner of
a shadowy room.
I would like to address myself to
parti-colored parrots
dead in tropical heat.
I would like to stroke the hood
of a speeding car.
I would very much like to gather up
an explosion.

THIS MAN INSISTING UPON LIVING

How can I leave you with only one?
If I give you nothing but that which I give
what will protect you? Is this, do you think,
only a rationalization, because I want to live?
Is my heart as black as this typing ink?
But I cannot leave you with only one!

No, no, no! Nor can I leave you
with only these, stamped and stamped, only these
    two:
nor could I leave you with more if I had any more;
no, not with three, if it were that three
were here for me to leave, or
even if I were lucky and had . . .
but I cannot leave you with only two.

Nor could I dream of
leaving you with only these three.
How would you survive;
how could you ever get along?
I must leave you with at least four.
Do you think that four will be enough?

No, I don't either; I'm sure you'll need more:
five at the very least, yes, at least five.
Oh, I am going to worry, worry so!
I had better re-think this.
Yes, I had better think more about this,
for how could I live with myself

if you didn't have enough to get by on?
Yes, it had better be six, or seven, ten perhaps,
and if I stay until tomorrow, I can, if I try,
make it twenty or thirty, a thousand—yes!
It must be a million: I must keep up my strength:
perhaps I had better not go: I'm so busy.

WINTER WAKING

Toward dawn
the ululation of an early dog,
amorous with the moon,
echoes hollowly from the hill,

and I turn over in my half sleep,
away from the new light,
away from the window,
into my pillow.

But the dog howls,
sounding lugubrious in his desire,
and sleep falls away
as I remember myself.

THE MAESTRO AND THE MESSENGER

I. The Maestro

Death, dark maestro of decay,
whose music numbs
your sorrow and dearly
purchased shame, says:

"Too late, too late!
Lie down and sleep,
my cloying clay;
oh, sweetly rest
in pieces, de rigueur.

"My smile
will lull you.
Bloodless, you'll lie
rank, severely ranked withal.
Feel how my music
is wet
or dry . . . ."

The maestro coughs,
taps his baton.
The symphony
he's mavening
begins . . . .

II. The Messenger

bicycled by,
his glistening bones
still wet with meat
   and wearing only

(immodest stick!)
a graveyard veil
of camouflage:
   "Wait, Mister! Wait!

I am trying to tell you,
I am trying to tell you . . ."
But his bones fell apart,
   his bones fell apart!

THE FUTURIST

> *And Death shall have no dominion . . .*
> *—Dylan Thomas*

And then we must replace you, Death, for you must go
with the combustion engine down the tube of time
and all will laugh at you as they do now at blimps
and bleeding, flapping wooden wings for flight and
   leeches
on the back for purifying blood, for in the future,
   Death,
hiatus will replace you, the storage called cryonics,
the deep freeze, or some such method to define
and discipline ourselves, to give a shape to time
and render meaningful our lives as you do now,
O wisdom-wasting Death, when life is lived poetically,
in many stanzas, each building on the last, developing
its theme, so that an open-sequence poem of life
is lived and not a golden drop of honey-wisdom
   wasted
that cost us generation after generation,
O Future, in long darkness climbing into you.

LIFE, A WESTERN

The dark matter of the universe
is that which filled the void
after the Big Bang, the smoke
of black powder swirling from the barrel
of Billy the Kid's six-gun.

Who exploded this dark dust?
Who squeezed the trigger on the universe?
How many must lay dead
before the Kid will holster
his garrulous gauche gun?

Si, amigo, this is the disease;
but never mind the cure;
let us learn a lesson from the cause.
The lesson is that to be born
is mighty good, but do not draw

on one so fast. But no! Draw!
And when you die with a neat
black hole in your bleeding heart,
fan the hammer as you fall
and bite the dust.

POETRY

puts a foot
on the back
of philosophy
and a foot
on the back
of science
and enjoys
a wild ride
stuntrider
never failing
to note
a prominence
in the
passing scene
always
wise enough
to put
both feet
on one
when they get
too far
apart
patient
to see them
re-team
satisfied
with every sight
and sound,
feeling
often

that the
eternal
factor
is the ride
itself
the rough
bucking ride
among the stars

HOUDINI AND THE DYING SWAN

Where was he? Was it a tunnel?
But he had come to a wall,
a slimy, wormy wall.
He must break through.
He must break out.
He felt for a tool.

Naked, she lay back in the tub,
white as a white swan, long-necked
as a swan, thin as a silken thread,
her gloriously thick dark hair
piled loosely up, collapsing
onto her wide, sloping shoulders,
dark, water-dipped ringlets forming,
her swan's-down skin pinking,
steam misting her swan song,
her suicide with water and razor.

II

They concentrated. A glittering
company. Rich. Celebrated.
They waited for the great Houdini.
His monument was dark, unmoving.
The stars glittered, like the company.
Half a minute. They breathed
in short, shuddering breaths,
and waited. Houdini heard:

"Houdini, do not disappoint us,
for we must believe that Death
cannot take us, utterly."

*Tearing at the wall, his long
yellow fingernails cracked off,
ricocheted; then he heard:
"I am dying, dying . . ." He drew back,
prepared to throw his body at the wall
--he must break through . . .*

III

The steaming water in the marble tub
was streaked in ribbons of red.
She was going to die, that *he* would know,
her lover, what he had done.
He had killed beauty
in neglect and pursuit of money.
He would be sorry. Her long lashes locked.
It was like a dream, and she was falling,
falling over a dark sea, which now she struck.
The noise jolted her. It was like
breaking plaster, like tumbling bricks,
like an earthquake. Her eyelids rolled back
to see a mad-eyed specter
emerge from a great, gaping hole
torn through tiles. Her dizzy mind,
half-bloodless, saw the bloodless form,

and fainted. Houdini lifted her from
the marble tub and taped her wrists.
He put her in her bed and tugged
the bell pull. She was too beautiful to die.
A great grandfather clock obliterated
the last of midnight. A doorknob turned,
and he went back the way that he had come.

Houdini darkened into death.

INCIDENT

The day is a blown and bending one.
The sky is puffs and smears.
The street is coats like flags
and wind-pushed faces,
eyes, isolation and confusion.
At the wild square
the flocking birds eye me,
move in little rushes.
A metal man, a hero, stands braving the wind,
unfeeling. I sit at his feet.
Near me a man seats himself,
then a thin girl, another man:
suddenly there are many, a crowd.
Across the square, in phalanx,
march men. They wear one earring each.
They are armed with small silk squares.
My group stands at attention, hums.
The phalanx halts. A man steps from it,
strikes the thin girl with the silk.
She is prostrate, bleeding.
One by one they step forward,
strike, and one by one they fall.
The last is struck. The hum has stopped.
The phalanx marches off.
I sit alone; begin to hum;
look at the hero.

ON WHEELS

Once, in a mind, and many times again, a wheel
rolled overland toward a far horizon, a wheel
twinned with another on a wooden pole, then
four wheels turned overland toward some always
West, grinding eternal ruts in time. A wheel
attired, a formal wheel, became four tires
in white-walled best, spinning overland toward
the setting sun, a white-hot wheel, a round thing
in the mind. Some wheels fall flat and spin, and
some stand up. Wheels chipped and put together
make up gears. A gear is just a chipped wheel in
a mind free for a moment from the threats of time.
A wheel is a round rock turned on its edge.
A wheel is just a round thing in a mind.

MINIM

art
out of
the
small
end of
the
hose
like
a
water
saw
can
chisel
stone
or
cut
steel

like
laser
light
narrowed
to
pluck
bad
blood
from
an eye
can
be
very
useful
&
good

HUSH, HUSH, NEW HOUSE IN CHARLOTTE

Our new old house climbs a hill,
backside sagging on stilts, porch chinning up
the short front lawn's long shaggy grass.
The hill drops down darkly behind the house.
Our eye-hooked back door isn't safe,
the basement a wedge of black cheese
for a great, grinning rat. Trees,
with octopus roots and upward tentacles, tap the
   roof.
The floors slant, decks frozen in a pitch.
As to the furnace, it groans, goes on,
and heat hisses up from floor vents. Off,
say a word in one room and you hear it in another,
pad about and it sounds from somewhere else.
The former tenant was old and mad as bees.
He shot at shadows with a Magnum,
out back, down there, in the tarpool.
He blew them out of the night, usually.
By day he walked out naked, hating neighbors.
He had the house boarded up, from inside,
and kept two sleek Dobermans. The kennel
lurked in the black cheese-wedge down there,
made out of all the inside doors in the house.
We broke it up, put the doors back on their hinges,
and now can smell them, doggy and dangerous.
That first was our initiation night:
up the back steps: pumpf, pumpf, pumpf, pumpf!
My daughter woke my mother, who woke my other
   daughter,
and they listened by the basement door. Pumpf!

six-footed, three-throated Fear flew to us,
my wife and I, and banged on our bedroom door.
"What is it? What did you hear?" "Pumpf, pumpf,
   pumpf!"
I hoped it was the heat, or our own feet,
padding about, leaping from the vents.
I went to the basement door, nevertheless,
and yelled down, "I've got a gun!" Pumpf!
I yelled down, "Get away while you can!"
Pumpf! I pushed open the basement door,
snapped the switch, and darkness disappeared.
We're home now. We've had our first fear.

ALLEGORICAL FOUNTAIN

Upon the Rock of Insolence
stands the Accuser,
a child. He is looking at the Accused,
pointing a finger,
shouting in a voice of watery music
that he himself
will never grow up.

The accused
has round eyes of love
for the Accuser.
He would walk back down
the leaden years
to be at his side
upon the Rock of Insolence.

THE PERUVIAN APPARITION

Thousands of people saw this occur, saw
the Madonna come down and go back into the sun.
I myself took a photo which came out pure gold.
I sent it to the National Geographic. Back

it came with a rejection letter, the substance
of which was that the photo editor could see
nothing in a Kodachrome of gold. The Madonna,
I wrote back, was herself pure gold, and I

myself saw her come down from the sky, and ducked,
like thousands of Peruvians who ducked that day,
at sight of this wonderful apparition.
But my letter was to no avail.

I keep my square of gold pinned on the wall.

A REPLY

When the wind blows down the house we thank the Lord
    that we were out that day; or, when the sea
turns our mast under its swashing opaque belly,
    and we are thrown clear, we swim and pray
thanksgiving, thanksgiving, selfishly forgetting
    that, like so many bits of bait, our brothers
twirl downward in the darkness, being bitten and
    consumed
    —but when you say you are an atheist,
then qualify that you're a rationalist as well,
    you say to me your reason's on vacation.

For all we know, there *is* a God, a chemist,
    and we are the byproducts of experiment,
luckily unknown to the great creator,
    who, if that creator were to learn of us,
might draw from a vast laboratory a sterilizer
    and spray us from the surface of the earth.

We don't know what or why we are, my epistolary
    friend,
    only that we are and we can think,
and with this small equipment we can challenge
    existence,
    that it not best us for a time, at least.
For each of us can triumph for a time, even the unborn
    has spent some positive force in first
dividing against the inertia of matter, a tiny Knight
    against the Dragon of Death, or unaliveness,
a dust adumbrating itself against the odds.

THE LESSON

I have learned not to be quiet,
otherwise Death finds you.

I have learned to be unstill,
to sit loud, to talk long.

And I have learned why some
of us go on mountain treks

and others leap, on motorcycles,
a dozen cars; but I have not,

anymore than these, been able
to sit silently still, and die.

A PILE OF LEAVES

They lose their scent,
that freshness of
beginning, but
something replaces it,
some odor on the air
out of the eternal
olla podrida of
decay, a gift,
folded in dimensions
not yet understood,
tied with the
string theory,
bowed and ribboned
with a Monarch's
living wings. They
tap the earth,
dissolve into pure
spirit—of leaves,
of cells, of atoms
—and return,
bodiless angels,
to the place from which
all is projected,
where intelligent
spirits prepare
for new flight,
the old injuries
understood,
assimilated,
forgiven.

THE SECRET AGENT

I am an agent for the stone
and the dust, I am an agent for the quanta
who have sent me here to buy them answers.
They want to know what they are
and why they have the jumping disease,
they want to know why they cannot rest;
when they fill the flowers, the flowers speak,
they shout in the full spectrum of colors,
they want to know what they are doing,
they want to know why, when they are comfortable
and blowing in a fine breeze, they are assaulted,
they want to know why they wither and die.

I am an agent for the water
and the ice and the steam, tell me
what they need to know, tell the Earth
why it hurtles, tell the moon why it follows,
tell the sun why it burns,
tell the universe why it is black
and full of fiery suns,
tell the suns what they are.

I have come here to buy answers.
I will pay with the flowers' colors,
with the birds' feathers, with Hope's breath.
Give me the price for my answers.
Name it, and the day will give you its light.
Name it, and the atoms will charge it.

I am an agent for a principal
that can afford to spend a million stars.

SPRING AND THE BLACK HOLES

When green things grow, in glowing spring,
I attend to nature for a time, dreaming
that there is meaning, something, beyond
what I can tell, not merely the Heaven and Hell
of whirling galaxies, not Byron's dreamless sleep,
or merely to be part of the dust that swirls,
and someday to be sucked in, as by
a celestial vacuum cleaner, a black hole,
into a what? another universe, still dust?
A what? The soul must be my vademecum
or life and spring become intolerable.

But I am trapped, caught in the trap of life,
the spring of death. Yet it's not death
which is the worst pain of my soul:
it's *rerum natura*, it's the black holes,
it's the not knowing, not being allowed,
which *is* allowed even in bright spring,
even in prime spring when green things grow.

And suppose there is no dreamless sleep? Suppose
we wake somehow to feel again
and what we feel is endless pain,
pain of time and space being born,
birthpang of stars, the spaceless yet infinite
pain of the black holes, where time, perhaps,
runs backward, or, worse, does not run at all,
but leaves your shadow magnified stiff,
frozen forever, upon its lip,
while every molecule, still

sentient, is smoked and rayed apart,
while still, while still, though somewhere else,
green things grow, in glowing spring.

IT MUST HAVE BEEN THE ANGELS

on the head of the pin who wrote the Bible
on the grain of rice, it must have been
a tulipful of minimalists who painted the rainbows
on the dew-drops, it must have been the microwave
that sang so hot from deep inside.

I know that the bee sees a different flower,
patterns and colors I can't see;
and I can imagine the million neon cells
of the octopus, that colorfully advertizes for love
or shyly vanishes before one's fascinated eyes,
or the corncobs of scent-cells in my sniffing,
trotting mutt's curious, streetwise nose.

I believe it had to have been
the angels on the head of the pin
who wrote the Bible on a grain of rice.

SPRING RIDES

It is like this now at the end of winter.
The poor trees have survived, like
the poor blacks and the poor whites
along the highway, who wave as you fly by.
They have survived another long winter.

Now suppose someone in a passing car,
someone very rich, were to heave from the car
a suitcase filled with money,
then in spring the trees would spend it
on new clothes and the little girls
would be wearing fresh leaves and flowers
on a breezy church day and would look "like a
    million"—
Well, there you have the waiting trees with their tight
    buds.

It is like that now at the beginning of warmth.
I have been waiting, like a willow for the wind,
hanging loose but useless, for the busy world outside,
though I have run my leagues and burned my wheels
waiting for winter to haul out—for here is not Aspen
down the slopes but a pickup stuck in a bog—
and now my drive is full of Flowering Judas,
and older today I feel younger than yesterday
and for no real reason am convinced of tomorrow.

BRING US A RAY

Is it any wonder
that shadows pray
to the moon?
The fall of darkness
kills the shadows!
Have you not seen
the shadows, late
afternoon, lift
their hands in defense?
They know what's coming.
They are aware
that they are going
to be overwhelmed.
But still, but still,
if they pray
to the moon
and the moon
has enough strength
left in it, a second-hand
cast may swoop down
to the multitude
of shadows, myriad
ghostly shadows now,
fearing extinguishment.
So the fading shadows pray,
Bring us a ray,
bring us a ray
to live by, Luna,
one-faced sun-mirror,
in this our saddest hour.

WALKIE-TALKIE

I admit my presentation isn't tops,
but I have been assured that You ignore
that kind of thing and go right to the spirit,
that You're interested in the heart of the matter,
as well as the matter of the heart—flesh,
but what dances it too.
                        So, if I ask,
do I offend? But before I ask, You know,
so do I offend even before I ask, am I
offensive by nature? My nature *is* nature's,
what am I to do? You know me to be turning
a corner before I go out for a walk.
Maybe You have a brick waiting for me there.
Maybe a divine breath has wobbled it, just
a little, and now, as I go by, down it falls.
Maybe it misses. Then it was just a warning,
right? But if it hits, I'm home free—no?
Please tell me the right way to go!

Now, please, pay attention to my list.
I don't need to read it out loud to You.
I don't need to say it inside my head.
If You deign to know, You already know.
Is the list too long? It's all about life.
Well, You know that. Why do I say it?
You know what we all want. But we want
the wrong things, don't we? And we get
what we really need—yes? So I don't
have to ask, I don't really have to pray.
I'll get what's coming to me, won't I?

"BATTER MY HEART . . . "

I, John Donne, poet, priest, and sinner,
upon seeing two things which emanated
into creation by human misuse and by the mis-
conception of the body's termination as death,
by bearing the one, learned that the other
could then painfully invade even virtue's heritage
of unsullied and everlasting life. First,
I grew ruinous and out of harmony, having
had imperfect faith, and, secondly, suffered
melancholia and dejection, proving my heart
to be mere clay and divested of the spirit.
For I understand myself as being mere walls of clay,
condensed, then scattered, dust, and, being so,
so also am I sacrilegiously already half wasted,
in that I half wasted my body in youth, and
in that now my gray-shrouded time is almost gone.
But, nonetheless, increase Your flame within me,
Your flame which produces tears of repentance,
and let that flame so rush out through my flesh,
even if it causes agony, that it goes everywhere,
and that I may see it in everything.
Help me to approximate integration of power,
love, and knowledge, so that with these three
forces functioning in harmony, I may better know
and love You. And may the martyrs come to me
to beg that I continue to live my life, and not die
by my own hand, my own Dioclesian and persecutor,
so that I become a wholly living martyr deprived
of my death and final belonging. And if the Experts
do their best to interpret the Register of the Elect,

and to unravel my confusions, keep me mindful of
   the
flaw invested in them, and necessary to them, and
let me forgive them their love of knowing, and mine.
When this is heard, my ears are shut, for listener
and answerer are one in one. And while all are
joined in a universal choir, which is also a
meditation on on three things, viz., "hope, bear, and
   do,"
help me to seek renewal even in a short, gray space.

THE LOSS

When the blackbird stood on the chimney and called,
poking her beak at the clear blue ice of the sky,
I watched from inside the frame of an old wooden
   house
across from the once two-chimneyed house where she
   stood,
heard her cry crack the ice of the sky that day
from the wrongest of chimneys, the wrongest.
The bricks lay scattered next to the house.
The big nest of hay had blown away.
The ugly babies now lived in the barn,
but for one, who had drowned in the well.

MORNING NOTES

I. *NEW DAY NEWS*

Early morning of a new day
squirrel-chirp loud outside the window
   five in the morning
coffee fresh & good
watching for the new light visitation
up the edge of the globe
   six o'clock
pale blue & dark green
defining the tree-horizon
vast, oncoming time—inevitability
   Hubble sees two galaxies collide
they look like an auto wreck in space
lots of flash & fire
   new suns
my wife sleeps late in warm sheets
dreaming of something, I suppose
my mood is perfect, quiet, thoughtful
   yet not fully awake, aware
when that comes
   everything goes
the day rolls out its red carpet
   & we all begin to walk it.

II. Aubade

It's Earthgodown & the sun fringes the horizon,
    lightening the sky.

As the crickets fall silent & the new day sings through
    the birds,
as the squirrels chirp for conversation & business, I
    open my eyes
to light & the din of morning awakenings, glad to be
    alive,

full of pleasure at time that has given me these
    phenomena,
this morning variousness that includes the percolation
    of the pot

of coffee in the kitchen that my wife has beaten me to
    making—
& rise with the metaphysics of morning to a day gone
    by
that I shall remember with much fondness on the
    morrow,

should I awaken to yet another Earthgodown, bird-sing
    & squirrel-chirp
of a morning in the enchanted magic of eternity.

SEE/SAW

Some artisan has molded
all these leaves out
of bright red clay and
baked them into this
mound of smoking ashtrays
on the lawn. I watch
my neighbor toss
his cigarette into
the burning mound,
and remember laws
against both smoking
and leaf burning
enacted here of late,
and think these may
be all the leaves
I see go up in smoke,
if virtue gets the best
of us, as it is wont
to do, until defeated
once again by our
rebellion, due in
turn eternally, and
here tomorrow if out
today. Our lives do not
so much improve as
see-saw with our wills,
and we clean up and
then we dirty up,
delighting in both
order and disorder

in their turns. I'd
wait for us to get it
right, if I had time.

INSTANT ANGELS

Thunder
    & lightning
        & downpour!

My clothes beat against me
like whirling laundry,

but I may never see angels again,
a myriad of instant angels

with transparent wings
appearing/disappearing

on the black asphalt
of the gleaming street,

all wings in a funnel,
like transparent butterflies

landing on black flowers;
but their long funneling wings

are of water.

NEW YEAR NEAR THE HUDSON

    The summit of time has been reached!
   Wind is the breath of the demon of ice
who breathes down our necks at the peak.

    In cold blood, with wide hands,
   he pushes, creeping and cresting dark water,
while across the rumpling bay,

    beyond illuminated, skyline geometry,
   while frozen excelsior hangs fire in the air,
a shuddering ragged phalanx

    traces the fall of a ball,
   as the polluted Hudson,
drunk on party poisons, rolls on.

INSECT SONG

Sing, downfalling measure!
Dog-day cicada, sing!

Oh, don't let up,
stout fellows, Falstaffs,
fat, winged knights!
I was losing myself
in your music. Sing on!
Give us the belly laugh,
the long vibrating call!

Sing on, grasshopper!
Harvest fly, sing on!

There's a harvest moon,
and many a star.

Night wind shucks the corn.

Webs are weaving.

Rain is coming.

Sing on! Sing on!
You harvest flies!
You katydids!
Sing for your ladyloves!
Sing for the sad world!

Leap to the bar, cricket!
The crescendo! The mad song!

BAD NEWS

tonight (and with gleeful
   morbidity, going on
to give us a variety
of unuseable deaths
disasters mayhem murder)

But the question is
why do we need them
   "It's what you thrill to,"
wrote Lawrence, *"and if you
thrill to rape, murder . . ."*

It is inside us,
the ancient
crocodile down deep
its eyes opening, closing
its jaws aching

Ah yes, bad
news tonight
folks (and our
ears perk up,

our noses twitch,
smelling blood)

TRUMPETS OF DOOM

Like an elephant's trunk,
    cut off,
my poetry trumpets blood
    out of anger,
as memory is drained
in each hoarse music,
    trumpets blood,
like an elephant's trunk,
    cut off,
for the helplessness
  of the mutilated,
telling the dark history
of the ivory poacher's greed
    and machete
that felled the musical beast
  in a trade for money,
  potency for the limp,
  the erotic for the dull,
but is merely the dust
    of the dead.
Like an elephant's trunk
    cut off,
my poetry trumpets blood,
  telling dark history.

DIALOGUE OF THE SUICIDE AND THE SMOKER

Ash on an old man's sleeve
Is all the ash the burnt roses leave.
                      —T.S. Eliot

"Look at you," said Müller,
who taught psychology,
and later committed suicide
when implicated in war crimes.
A vegetarian, he picked
at his salad and eyed Smith
with distaste. "You have ashes
down the front of your shirt.
It is a dirty habit, smoking.
And I see you always drinking
in that cocktail bar by the
lake. You must take better
care of yourself, Smith."

"Worry is what kills you.
I grade papers there. It's
very pleasant—a beautiful view,
even in winter, when the lake looks
like a bowl of liquid iron. You
know, in 1496, Romano Pane,
a monk who accompanied Columbus,
became the first person to
describe the tobacco plant
to the old world. Tobacco
was brought from America

to Spain in 1555. In 1560,
the tobacco plant was imported
to Western Europe by Jean Nicot;
hence, nicotine. It brought
pleasure and pain, as all things do."

"How do you know such things
—dates like that, I mean?"

"I look them up. They're
comforting, definite.
Very little is." "You appear
detached." "Not detached.
Perhaps transcendent. Sir
John Hawkins introduced
tobacco into England
in 1565. That was the same
year that pencils began
to be manufactured there.
Also, Sir Thomas Gresham
founded the Royal Exchange
in London, same year. And
the Knights of St. John,
under Jean de La Valette,
defended Malta from the Turks.
The Turkish siege was broken with
the arrival of Spanish troops."

"What's the difference?"
"Exactly! Erskine Caldwell

published Tobacco Road in 1932.
Jack Kirkland's play version
of TR opened to a long run
in New York in '33. But
at the end of the century
I have to go outside to smoke,
and the autumn wind blows
the ashes all over me."

"I should like my ashes
to be scattered over the lake,"
Müller said. Smith lit another
cigarette, watched the smoke
scurry off in puffs and strands.
"I'll see to it," he said.

BRAVE NEW WORLD

Skyscrapers stand empty
or are turned into
hydroponic plants.

No capitols,
pure dislocation!

Nations have turned into
fluent electronic collectives
with citizens scattered as stars.

THE HONEY HOUSE

With its white picket fence and its little green lawn
and its rose bushes over here and over there in bud,
it was a picture book, a *Post* cover, a dream, of a house.

And it was theirs! But there *were* a lot of bees, weren't
    there?
It was the rose bushes, the wisteria, the dogwood, it was
the sweetness of their young love. She was pregnant—

bad to be stung by a bee she was trying to bat away,
    then
stung by another. She ran from the house and he came
    home.
Why, there was a beehive under the kitchen sink!

Then he saw that five bees had lit at the top of his paper,
which he shook, and he dodged but was stung just the
    same,
and the buzzing was deafening, he said, deafening.

So they called in the Masked Exterminator, who dis-
    covered
that the house was filled with hives, ten feet tall in the
    walls,
right up through the floors. Didn't you see the honey?

Now in full summer the walls had begun to drip, the
    floors
oozed honey. Yours, said the Masked Exterminator, is
    a honeyhouse.

It's true, said the bride, I have washed it up and hosed it
    down.

And suddenly all were attacked and ran from the house.
Upshot: bride thought groom a fool and divorced him,
groom sued broker, who sought out former owner,

who had moved to Alaska, with intention of recouping,
supermarket tabloids did a number of stories on the
    house,
and, after her abortion, bride was invited to pose for
    Playboy.

THE SOULS

Outside on a green lawn a giant water-oak conducts a
   sunset.
   Some unsteady hum has summoned us out of our
      houses.
My ancient lady friend, who lives nearby, is jawing
   now, and wears
   an awed-holy expression as she says they are souls,
      yes sir.
And they are everywhere, they wade the dusky clouds,
   they are
   giant black-winged fruits hanging, falling, bouncing.
      The green
is black with them. And neighbors stare; they worry for
   their

cars and pickups. If they get into the red berries, it's
   hell on
   paint. Shoot them. No, they are beautiful. They are a
      menace.
Look out below! They rise and wheel, kaleidoscopic,
   inside rings
   of themselves. They set themselves against the sky,
      black on blue.
They caw. They are telling themselves, or us,
   something.
   They caw and caw, and what is it they are saying, so
earpiercingly, holes through your eardrums, through
   your brain,

as if lasered? Then they settle again, like a black
   blizzard

of huge coal flakes. The souls come back to visit us,
   to tell
us that they know everything now. Now their sharp
   yellow beaks
   pierce the lawn. They are busier than worms, in a
     feast
of famishment, an ecstasy of appetite. Now, she says,
   the nonagenarian, I'll soon be with them, and then
it's always now for me like them. The souls have found
   their

bodies. I don't know which is which, but somewhere,
   there,
   is everyone who died, all the loved ones, and even the
     others,
the ones that nobody loved, they are all there now, she
   says.
   I stare as deep as I can see. They are every blessed
place—on roofs, looking down, in trees, on bushes,
   under,
   over, and around. Some seem to be waiting, some tug
at the turning-emerald lawn in the lowering light: and
   now

how do they know to rise suddenly, and become one
   wide
   black wing? How do they know to circle and circle in
     unison,
one boomerang black wing composed of so many
   blood-beating,

   sky-rowing black wings? How do they know when
      it's time
to fly along a horizon, rimmed with rising red? The
   souls,
   they know, they know! I think it must be out of some
      distant
folklore that the old lady speaks, eyes fixed, waving
   them goodbye.

OVER THE MAGNOLIA

You want to know
what the moon
tells the wolf,
so at night
you lie in bed
and hold the crystal
ball you bought
at the novelty
store, hold it up
beside the moon,
which is right
outside the window,
over the magnolia,
and howl very
softly, so as
not to wake
anyone, growl
under the lips-
high blanket, and
beg mercy of
the moon.

BECAUSE

in the port-cities they have found everything out and
Aristotle-like have put everything into categories
and the unicorn is an ungulate because they say so
because the fine-print of the unreligious sun says we
    circle it
it is not for us but we for it because the moon hit us
and bounced off instead of was born of our first spin
because the ninth planet is an invading comet caught
and because there is no now and there never has been

because we look upon ourselves in savannas past
knuckling to water because we see the white lemming's
    hole
in the snow smashed down by hooves and hear its pitiful
chirp of counter-aggression because the avalanche
indifferently buries the contested world of the snow
valley because stars die because we believe in facts
and because the deluge led to the ark because because
and because we bury our dead and dig up their bones

because the unsoundness of our judgments lead to sound
judgment and because facts are facts and we must reckon
and because the sea is cruel and because time flies
because the wind blows down our houses and because
we remember the snow hare and the hawk because
because the dove is taken in air by the eagle
and because space is either empty or full of dark matter
because galaxies hold for a long time their pinwheel
    shapes

because time and space are curved and we can blow
    ourselves up
and because we blow ourselves up constantly and
    because
it makes us wonder because doesn't it mean something
because we are riding a mud-ball through space because
we were born here and because we have categories and
because we dig up our bones and dogs dig our bones up
and because we are not even safe in pyramids because
we dig ourselves up and look upon our own bones

THE NEW

It has always been so,
that species were endangered,

indeed, that they died out,
but it has also always been so,

that they evolved into the life,
new animals, not birds that fly,

but burrowers but not moles, etc.,
and I wish I might be able

to wait for the one I have in mind,
the one with no body, the one

made of spirit, a nebulous
laughing creature, a music

of a thing, which I have faith
is somewhere out there, coming.

PART SIX

COMMENCE FIRE!

2300 folding chairs on the lawn,
relatives with an actuarial average
of 30 years left in them,
fathers less, mothers more,
and grandmothers more than ever
(I hasten to add, non-smokers
more than anyone), myself
hot on a warm June day:
commencement socializing:
1888: Lover's Leap and
Hold-Me-Tight buggies: today
expensive sports cars
for the kids, up to limousines for
the relatives. The campus
is crowded with vehicles, gleaming
colors abound: chauffeurs
stand in clusters of uniforms, smoking.
I envy them. Grads with an actuarial life
of 50 years ahead of them,
maybe 60, sweat with heat
and excitement, caps and gowns,
and in anticipation of booze,
dancing, prancing, and romancing
tonight: but first, ROTC
commissioning, Baccalaureate
Service, Supper with the
school President and his wife
(parents and their students are urged
to remain on campus for Supper),
Open Houses, faculty and staff

homes, a concert by the college choir,
a Jazz ensemble. There won't be a
hotel or motel room empty
for a radius of 50 miles.
I scan young faces in the hope
that some of them know
the difference between fancy
and the imagination,
between a Baccalaureate and
a Bacchanalia, between
an apposable behind and
a prehensile tail, etc.
Orator fit, poeta nascitur.
Poeta nascitur, non fit.
I'm halfway into the wrong
racket. Bon voyage, and
vaya con Dios, my darlings!

OLD ICARUS

Grandchildren turning
their faces from
drooling kisses
to avoid
what you have
become:
teeth like graveyard
stones, sunken cheeks
pockmarked
(where once,
as a boy,
the feathers went),
wens, wild hairs.

The wax your father poured
has melted
and the feathers,
plumes he placed so carefully,
flew, fell,
and you fell
into the sea
but did not drown,
owning a future,
as you did,
long enough
to hug your grandchildren
close and have them
turn away.

BALDING

When these blow-dried twigs
finally fall, or are deracinated,
tangled in some last, accomplished comb,
or in the glib fingers of a lover
fine-boned and sharp-nailed enough

to play tweezers, the scarred skin
will gleam nakedly in the mirror,
burnished by sun and overhead bulb
and, quick as life, we shall have been
transformed into a meditative monk,

skull-capped and burnoosed, who
belongs to the Monastery of Maturity,
and bears on his weary shoulders,
silently, to his last small cell,
his own *memento mori*.

GIN RUMMIES

> *To find a friend one must close one eye.*
> *To keep him—two.*
> *Norman Douglas*

for Rodney Formon

Friday nights, a fry-cook,
arms scarred by sizzling fat,
Rodney bangs on my door.
We like to drink together,
shoot the shit, and laugh.
Drunk enough, we sing!
It's karaoke with CDs scattered
on the table, improvisational
shandygaffs and combinations
you can't enjoy with your relations.

   It's good to have a drinking buddy.
I've used up two already—
one who fell down a flight of stairs
and one, who was much older,
who died of his warrior life.
But now I've got Rodney,
who is very different from the others.

The other two were quite and somewhat
intellectual, and where the one
could talk history or science, art,
music, or just about any subject
in just about any language and come back,

being polyglot, and polymath,
even polymorphic, after hooch,
the other was a man of action,
a war hero with many medals
tucked away in drawers locked
by indifference, but still would tell of
weapons, arms and the man, and such
with fervor—my Heraclitus—
and also with disgust, with
fatalism, believing nothing
changes in man's fighting nature,
disposed to think the worst;
but enthusiastic over chess,
which he played in earnest
as if he were at war again.

   But Rodney is another sort:
He knows I write but will not read
a word I write, nor much else either,
but likes the Internet so much
he slides crabwise in thought,
toward what depth of cyberspace
I often cannot fathom until *zing*
I see it for myself, or am I drunk?

   I see with Rodney that the other two,
complimented first my young and then
my middle-aged delusions
of a deeper self-knowledge
than available to most. Yes, Rodney

shows me to myself, or shows me
to my youthful ghosts, as ego-fed,
but did and does this unintentionally,
whose wonderful indifference makes me shrink
like a cock in the cold, and chug my drink.

CHRONICLE

Out of the mustard tang that filled my mouth
with the vivid day once when wind
brought itself riffling through my short golden mane
like the hand of God being the cub's mother's tongue
came that time when life was endless wonder
and listening to the wind take away laughter
as a chime with wings as little silver
stars afloat like darting butterflies
as sipping hummingbirds at one long meal
within that wind on such wide wings
as monarchs never know nor hummingbirds
but boys and girls flying their youth
wantonly was my dear time wasted
and now it is bells for a stopped watch
where I have ground my teeth out
my novel of ten thousand pages
empty as my mouth.

PROVENANCE OF AN OLD POET

for Stanley Kunitz

Today he strolled the park,
seeing babies and their bright
new mothers, and he thought
of death, but not depressingly,
just as a fact of life, because
birth makes the old mark
how time is running out.

Then, too, he thought of provenance—
proof of birth, the papers
going with an antique,
or work of art—which was the word
which prompted him to start
a park-bench verse to relatives,
friends, and to the world in general
—distant friends, he guessed
you could call them, just to say
how far back his parchments go
—to Europe, Asia, Africa, even
to the great Oneland, Gaea,
and perhaps beyond—it could be
that they started at God's waving hand,
and came down from Bango.

All this youthful joy
has made him think of how,
when he was young,

he loved to go dancing
to the Big Bands.

He could dance the legs off ladies
who were willing to swing
until the stars came out
and the dawn star shown once more.
These young mothers were like them.

Well, as the great globe goes,
tonight will bring him
the Starlight Ballroom back,
with enough documents,
validations,
certificates,
provenance,
viz., tickets,
to allow him to dance
between the starry poles
in a not unfriendly universe.

HIRE ACTORS!

Being superficially
mourned would be a
last wicked joke on me.

Hire actors

who, though they have
never met me, can
read my story and
genuinely feel.

Hire actors

and be honest and
revile me at leisure
while the actors mourn.

Hire actors

who have been taught
the Method and know
their motivations.

Hire actors!

One good actor can feel
more than an average
family.

Hire actors!

THE NURSING HOME

There are more women than
men in the nursing home and
more men than old doctors.

Staff doctors visit once a
month. The few old men do
very little but sleep. Two

or three of them occasionally
gather outside in clear
weather for a smoke, which

is allowed them. I suppose
those in charge feel that
it can make no difference

now, and it brings the old
men a little pleasure. I
sit and chat with them

sometimes. Perhaps "chat"
is a bit too lively a word
to describe what passes for

conversation during these
puffing sessions. A lot
of low grunting goes on.

There is one old man who
is afflicted with bone

cancer and who says, in

high good humor, that his
guarantees have run out.
He was a travelling salesman

in women's wear, and still
remembers how much he loved
women. Many of the women

have become little girls
again. They carry dolls
about with them, mostly

rag-dolls, I suppose so
they can't injure themselves
when they squeeze them.

To see these toothless,
balding old ladies, frail
as twigs, clutching these dolls,

is heartbreaking. Oh, to love
something! It's still there.
It has been in them since

they were little and had dirty
knees and bows in their hair.
Some recognize me now, and,

when I give them a wave,
they wave back. It's a
wonderful feeling to make

contact, but it is difficult
to tell how much they know.
The care-givers are kind and

efficient. They are mostly
young, and apparently try
to imbue the old with some of

their zest for life, but
of course the old know all
that already—or knew and have

forgotten it. I wonder,
can the young reverse their
situations with the old

and see themselves looking up
at such fresh faces from the
vantage of bed or wheelchair

or walker? I am too young
to join the old here in the
nursing home, this metaphor

(or is it the tenor of a
metaphor?) for the last days,

but I am too old

to feel the buoyancy of the
young; so, at least for the
context of the nursing home,

I have arrived at yet another
awkward age. After visiting
my mother, who is only partly

present, I go out and sit
with the old men and have a
smoke. We hope for clear days.

OUTSIDE THE HOSPITAL

The sentence of night, the comma-moon,
the asterisks and periods of light,
tell a tale of a great dark space.

And who is the writer of the night
tale, who is the author of hours
during which one waits for relief,

as the jangled nervous system mutely
screams, as the heavens revolve, as
your world waits to face the dawn?

THOSE WHO DIE IN THEIR SLEEP

When the mind is wakeful
and the eyes are shut,
ears buried in their pillows
hear the song and
then it fades behind them
as on a distant shore,
and some drown then
and can never hear again
the song of the dreaming mind
singing its own mystery,
but now the song of the non-
life of the non-mind, of
the stars wheeling to Nowhere,
of time ending, snuffing out
the stars, one by one, the song
of all that has never known
of its own existence.

NOW, THE FOX!

> *We suffer from reminiscences...*
> — *Karl Menninger*

   A thousand times I've had this urban dream &
asked a doctor what it meant
   to no avail. "It was the city's grip on
an impressionable child,"
   one doctor told me. I was dropped once down a
hellish, pitch-black pit, a deep
   dumbwaiter shaft, & fell a floor before I
landed, more or less intact.
   I bear a scar above my eye. Could that be
it, dropped by a drunken man,
   a family friend, when I was still an infant?
Meaning harmlessly to play,
   he swore off drink, I'm told. In any case I
have these nightmares constantly,
   & doubt if they will ever go away. Waking,
after one, I'm shaken to
   the bone. I live now in the country, where I
hoped to find diminishment
   of terror, over time. But here's the strange part:
rabies is a major threat
   here in the country in the summer—dogs &
cats can get it from the wild-
   life teeming in the woods—& just the other
night I dreamed a foaming fox
   that chased me back into the cityscape I
hoped so much to free myself
   from, years before, by coming to the country.

   Waking horror brought me new
      concern for peace of mind & where to find it.

OLD WOMEN, PAUSING

Old women, pausing, standing midblock on a hill
or midlevel on subway steps, waiting for breath,
their shopping bags hanging from toughened hands,
their eyes back in girlhood, perhaps, or ahead,
on the next meal, the contents of the bags
cooked and served, their honor again earned,
exist away from where they are, the grade or incline
slowly flattening, reversing, as their hearts calm
and their breath comes slower, more peacefully;
and so they stand, with the stillness of statues,
black-coated, black-shod, eyes straight ahead,
wisps of pale hair riffling slightly with the breeze,
waiting for breath, ahead of or behind where they are.
—So all of us, ahead of or behind where we are
or separated from what we are, not complete,
having left part of ourselves behind,
not having done that which we hoped to do,
not having attained to that which we hoped to attain,
all like old women, standing midblock on a hill,
waiting for breath, ahead of or behind where we are.

HEART FAILURE

I have made my moon landing at night
by way of the emergency ward,
on the strong black arm of a nurse.
My wife is the other woman,
and between the two women I enter,
seeing, reflected in glass, my red car
half up on a curb, and mal-angled,
the glare of the high beams showing
my terrified wife's confusion.

There is no air in that car,
there is no air in the night,
but there is air in the hose that the nurse
claps to my turning-blue face,
and strength in her arms that are used to
the harsh struggles that have plagued her
existence,
strength that I finally can share in.

I lie in a gown in a room,
and the silent killer says nothing.
He signalled, I guess, with red flags.
I paid no attention. I'd developed
an elephant's hide, an armor for the arrows
of insult that poor boys endure.
From childhood, when I was raw,
and my nerves could actually bleed,
I worked on this suit of armor,
oiled it and flexed it and shined it,
but now it belonged to them,

the doctors who probed me with wonder.
"Didn't you notice a thing?
You sound like a sidewinder, rattling."
"I thought I'd caught cold in the chest."
But I had no desire to know
because I had no desire to stop.
I could see that they thought, "What a fool!"
All but the black nurse, who knew
how the poor slid the slippery slope
that poverty, stress, and high blood pressure
grade for the struggling-upward.
She pulled at my ear, and said, "Tough guy!
He don't take no crap from his heart."
She knew how the pressure builds up,
as you climb in the ignorant ghetto,
until you would break, or be broken.

"How you doing, baby doll? Better?"
"Yes, but now I'm embarrassed."
—embarrassed at being so weak,
ashamed of my heart that can fail,
ashamed to have such a heart—
no lionheart, no Coreleone, I.
But they tell me it's stress that's at fault:
the heart is okay, the tests show.
The angel nurse flattens my hair,
pulls at my ear, and says, "Go!—"

DEATH

What do I know about death?
It is a question one must
occasionally ask oneself
Death who are you what are you
No metaphor will do
because that is merely
a likening of one thing
to another thing, which
when it comes to death
is impossible, for
death being unknown
anything we should
choose would be
arbitrarily chosen
and therefore
would be a bad
metaphor nobody
being able to say
how close or distant
the vehicle
from the tenor
the subject being
death. How then
do we approach this
unsubject this
antisubject this
but you see
even here
is a metaphor
even here

      we are at a loss
      that we are asking
      a question for which
      the only answer
      is death.

NAMES OF THE DEAD

The names of the dead sail on.
They are like white seabirds against a white sky,
then black seabirds against a black sky.
Every so often you hear the flutter of wings.
Into your ear comes a name.
That was Kaufman, you say.
Then a vague picture appears in your head,
at the back or in the front, against the walls.
You shake your head.
Maybe you see a smile different from others.
Long, narrow teeth in front. Kaufman.
The names of the dead sail on
like seabirds over the moony sea.

A MEMORY

for Ludwig Datené

Decades ago,
and decades ago,
under a sulphurous
night sky, in summer,
we sat on an asphalt
roof, looking up
at the dull stars,
like melting bronze,
overhead (& down
six floors a candle
in a bottle, melting),
smoking pot, saying,
dreaming young men
high over rubble,
that no matter what
we would not alter
but go on, you
to paint, I to write—
for, if we failed,
we'd have done
what must be done,
vowing dramatic youth.
My heart hurts
to remember
us so young.

EMANATION FROM THE PENUMBRA

Poets
of my generation
are turning up
dead. A serial
killer
is injecting
them
with cancer
heart disease
and stroke.
This police
silhouette
of the killer
isn't made
of his head,
but of his
twisted mind,
made
of a brain
to answer
for his crimes
of torture
perpetrated
on two friends.
With a rough
cat-tongue
he licked flesh
from bones
and made
the other
mercy-kill
to make
amends.
Look
from
a high bridge,
as highway god,
he drops
stones on old bones!
Even the sap
of trees is worried
up the trunk
as the killer
waits
for a weariness
of leaves.
I am
Time's agent
his tool
he brags.
My generation thinks
that this
is a serial crime,
but has
no choice
but to pull
the ropes
and toll
the bell

THERE I AM

Everyman, I will go with thee . . .

And there I go, stopping for a beer,
for several, and smoking too much.
There I am, laughing with the guys.
There they are, and we all look alike.
We tell one another about being in the service.
We tell one another about how bad the food was.
Some of us had never had better. There I go,
telling the same tired old dirty joke.
There I go again, for the umpteenth time,
and then I go, walking home to my wife.
I can see myself now. And there I am,
at the weddings, eating and drinking.
The tux is too tight now, the legs too short.
It's the same one I wore on the cake,
when I was the plastic man standing there
with the plastic bride in her white dress.
And there we are dancing at the VFW.
My stomach hangs over my belt.
And there I am with my gold watch.
And there I am with my first grandchild.
I am completely bald now. It's the chemo.
And I am thin again, my shoulders narrow,
but my hips have broadened; and there I am,
looking better than I have for years,
in my final repose, with the others looking at me
as if they had never seen me before,
calling me daddy and grandpa,
calling me husband, son, pal.

TOWARD THE END

One long winter at Revere Beach in Massachusetts,
with snow banked up two feet or more at the door,
I read Karl Marx's romantic tales from Dickens.
I discovered that the essence of that big tome
was somewhere in the first fifty pages,
where Marx gives out with his theory of value,
i.e., that the labor that is put into something
invests it with value. A flattering fallacy.
I had worked as a laborer much of my young life
and knew that if two hundred men moved a pile of shit
weighing two hundred tons two feet from its original
location—it was still a pile of shit.
Shovelling shit was something I knew about,
something you don't learn much about in the
reading room of the British Museum,
so Marx was a big disappointment to me.
And was it true that if God did not exist
everything was permissible, as in The Brothers
Karamazov? I went through the Great Books
of the Western World, the Cambridge Ancient Histories,
etc., etc., and in the end came to the conclusion
that all learning is meant to teach only one thing:
how little one knows. Now, in the face of the Great
   Dark,
I know that I know nothing—well, little of importance,
a few apparent facts, a wet paper bag full of information,
so, toward the end, now, though still seeking to under-
   stand,
I only read poetry or look up at the mysterious stars.

ABOUT THE AUTHOR

E.M. Schorb is a prize-winning poet and novelist. His 2016 *Dates and Dreams: Short Fictions, Prose Poems, Cartoons* was awarded the Writer's Digest International Self-Published Award for Poetry; a previous collection, *Murderer's Day,* was awarded the Verna Emery Poetry Prize and published by Purdue University Press; and his earlier collection, *Time and Fevers*, was the recipient of the Writer's Digest International Self-Published Award for Poetry and also an Eric Hoffer Award. Other works include *50 Poems,* Hill House New York, *Reflections in a Doubtful I,* White Violet Press, *The Journey and Related Poems,* Aldrich Press, *The Ideologues and Other Retrospective Poems,* Aldrich Press, *Eclectica Americana,* Hill House New York, and *The Poor Boy,* Dragon's Teeth Press, Living Poets Series. The title poem, "The Poor Boy," was awarded the International Keats Poetry Prize by London Literary Editions, Ltd., judged by Howard Sergeant. Schorb's novel, *Paradise Square,* received the Grand Prize for Fiction from the International eBook Award Foundation at the Frankfurt Book Fair. *A Portable Chaos* was the First Prize Winner of the Eric Hoffer Award for Fiction. But Schorb maintains that he is first and foremost a poet, and his poetry has appeared in numerous publications, here and abroad.

www.ingramcontent.com/pod-product-compliance
Lightning Source LLC
Chambersburg PA
CBHW031415290426
44110CB00011B/394